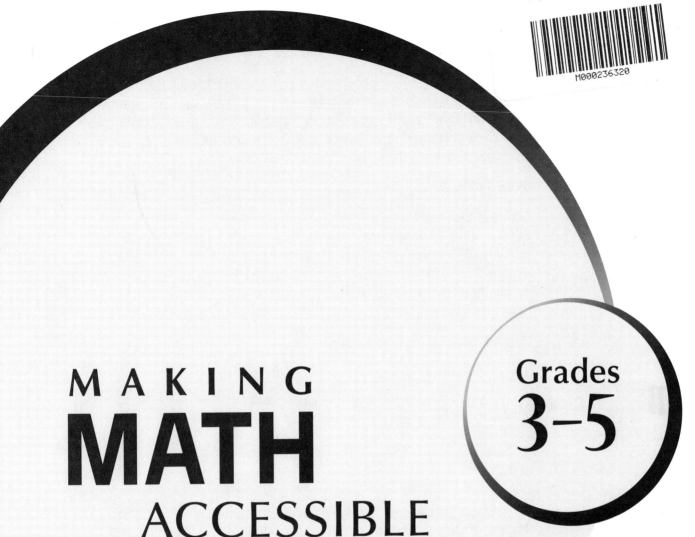

MAKING
MATH
ACCESSIBLE
to English Language Learners

Grades 3–5

Practical Tips and Suggestions

A Joint Publication

Solution Tree | Press a division of
Solution Tree

r4
Educated Solutions

Published by Solution Tree Press

555 North Morton Street
Bloomington, IN 47404
800.733.6786 (toll free) / 812.336.7700
FAX: 812.336.7790
email: info@solution-tree.com
solution-tree.com

Printed in the United States of America

13 12 11 10 09   1 2 3 4 5

FSC
Mixed Sources
Product group from well-managed
forests and other controlled sources
Cert no. SW-COC-002283
www.fsc.org
© 1996 Forest Stewardship Council

Library of Congress Cataloging-in-Publication Data
Making math accessible to English language learners : practical tips and suggestions, grades 3-5 / r4 Educated Solutions.
        p. cm.
    Includes bibliographical references and index.
    ISBN 978-1-934009-63-5 (perfect bound) -- ISBN 978-1-935249-16-0 (lib. bdg.)
1. Mathematics--Study and teaching (Elementary) 2. English language--Study and teaching (Elementary)--Foreign speakers. 3. English language--Study and teaching (Elementary)--Spanish speakers. I. R4 Educated Solutions.
    QA135.6.M355 2009
    372.7--dc22
                                        2009028315

President: Douglas Rife
Publisher: Robert D. Clouse
Director of Production: Gretchen Knapp
Managing Editor of Production: Caroline Wise
Copy Editor: Elisabeth Abrams
Proofreader: Sarah Payne-Mills
Text Designer: Orlando Angel
Compositor: Ron Wise
Cover Designer: Amy Shock

Acknowledgments

r4 Educated Solutions would like to acknowledge the dedication of the many Region 4 content-area specialists and external reviewers who devoted time to the development of this book. Their expertise and commitment to children produced this resource to assist educators with quality, effective classroom instruction for English language learners.

Visit **go.solution-tree.com/ELL** to download the reproducibles in this book.

Table of Contents

About r4 Educated Solutions

r4 Educated Solutions is a first-choice provider for the needs of educators, schools, and districts, from cutting-edge instructional materials to assessment data visualization, efficient food service training, and inventive transportation solutions. r4 Educated Solutions products and services are developed, field-tested, and implemented by the Region 4 Education Service Center (Region 4).

Region 4, located in Houston, Texas, is one of twenty service centers established by the Texas Legislature in 1967. The service centers assist school districts in improving student performance, enable school districts to operate more efficiently and economically, and implement state initiatives. Encompassing seven counties in the upper Texas Gulf Coast area, Region 4 serves fifty-four independent school districts and forty-nine state-approved charter schools. As the largest service center in Texas, Region 4 serves an educational community of over one million students (almost one-fourth of the state's total student population), more than 83,000 professional educators, and approximately 1,300 campuses.

The core purpose of Region 4 is revolutionizing education to inspire and advance future generations. Instructional materials such as this publication are written and reviewed by content-area specialists who have an array of experience in providing quality, effective classroom instruction that provides the most impact on student achievement.

Introduction

Most of us would probably agree that a major purpose of education is to develop each student's intellect so that reaching his or her career and social goals is a viable possibility. A vital component of that development is the ability to understand, participate, and communicate in the academic environment of the classroom. Students who lack the language skills required in the classroom are less likely to reach their goals. The purpose of this book is to help teachers accelerate the acquisition of the language skills needed by our English language learners (ELLs) to develop mathematics proficiency.

Changing Demographics

Nearly one in five Americans over the age of five speaks a language other than English at home. This statistic represents approximately forty-seven million people that live in the United States (U.S. Census Bureau, 2003). On the other hand, the latest Canadian census indicates that almost 3.5 million people, over 11 percent of the population, most often speak a nonofficial language at home—a language other than English or French (Statistics Canada, 2006). And the number of speakers of other languages in both countries is increasing.

More than one-fourth of the total population in some states speaks a language other than English at home, and the percentage of other language speakers increased dramatically in several additional states. Table I.1 (page 2) shows data from several selected states.

Table I.1: Individuals Speaking a Language Other Than English at Home (United States)

State	1990	2000	Percent Increase
Arizona	700,287	1,229,237	75.5
California	8,619,334	12,401,756	43.9
Georgia	284,546	751,438	164.1
Illinois	1,449,112	2,220,719	48.1
Nevada	146,152	427,972	192.8
New Jersey	1,406,148	2,001,690	42.4
New Mexico	493,999	616,964	24.9
New York	3,908,720	4,962,921	27.0
Oregon	191,710	388,669	102.7
Texas	3,970,304	6,010,753	51.4

Source: U.S. Census Bureau, 2003

The increase in the number of speakers of nonofficial languages is even more dramatic in Canada, largely due to the greater percentage of immigrants (see table I.2). In 1991, 214,200 immigrants entered Canada (Statistics Canada, 1994). In 2006, 1,109,980 immigrants entered Canada. The total immigrant population in 2006 was 6,186,950—one in every five Canadians (Statistics Canada, 2006). In the United States, one person in eight is an immigrant (Camarota, 2007).

Table I.2: Individuals Speaking a Nonofficial Language at Home (Canada)

Province	1991	2006	Percent Increase
Newfoundland	3,410	9,540	180
Prince Edward Island	2,700	2,960	9.6
Nova Scotia	10,800	34,620	221
New Brunswick	5,070	18,320	261
Quebec	399,970	886,280	122
Ontario	1,169,850	3,135,045	168
Manitoba	10,810	236,320	209
Saskatchewan	48,460	118,465	145
Alberta	196,010	583,530	198
British Columbia	328,210	1,091,530	233

Source: Statistics Canada, 2001

In U.S. schools in the year 2000, 16 percent of prekindergarten students were the children of immigrants, and only 2 percent were foreign born. However, in secondary schools, 19 percent of the total student population were children of immigrants, and 7 percent of students were foreign born. The larger number of foreign-born students at the secondary level presents exceptional challenges to schools since many foreign-born students enter school with limited English proficiency and, often, few years of regular education in their home countries (Capps, Fix, & Murray, 2005). Many of these students are not fully literate in their first language, much less in English (Ruiz-de-Velasco & Fix, 2000), and the period of instructional time available for these late-arriving students to achieve reading, writing, and content proficiency increases the pressure on schools to accelerate their learning, often without the additional funds for language programs provided to elementary schools (Batt, Kim, & Sunderman, 2005).

Tables I.3 and I.4 provide insight into the significant numbers of English language learners (ELLs) in several of North America's largest school districts.

Table I.3: Students Served in ELL Programs (United States)

School District	State	Percent of Students
Anchorage School District	Alaska	12.1
Tucson Unified District	Arizona	13.9
Los Angeles Unified District	California	43.8
San Francisco Unified District	California	28.4
Denver County	Colorado	29.9
Dade County	Florida	16.7
DeKalb County School District	Georgia	13.6
Boston School District	Massachusetts	19.0
Clark County School District	Nevada	21.2
Portland School District	Oregon	12.9
Dallas Independent School District	Texas	31.5
Houston Independent School District	Texas	28.9
Fairfax County Public Schools	Virginia	16.4
Milwaukee	Wisconsin	6.6

Source: National Center for Education Statistics

Table I.4: Individuals 5–19 Years Old Who Speak a Nonofficial Language at Home (Canada)

City	Province	Percent of Individuals
Edmonton	Alberta	17.2
Hamilton	Ontario	21.4
Montreal	Quebec	9.8
Toronto	Ontario	17.6
Vancouver	British Columbia	21.1

Source: Statistics Canada, 2006

These changing demographics take on even greater importance when we consider high school graduation rates. Almost 68 percent of dropouts in the United States—defined as 16 to 24 year olds who are neither enrolled in nor graduated from high school—were either foreign born or the children of foreign-born parents (Child Trends Data Bank, n.d.). According to Gunderson (2008), the numbers are almost as dismal for Canada, where the disappearance rate for English as a second language (ESL) students is approximately 60 percent, with speakers of Spanish, Vietnamese, Tagalog, or Punjabi representing the largest language groups in the disappearance rate. (Gunderson uses the term *disappearance rate* instead of *dropout rate* because of the lack of data to track which students have left the district and which students have permanently left school.) However, when the data are disaggregated, it becomes apparent that the graduation rate varies greatly with the subgroup. For instance, students whose first language is Chinese have a graduation rate comparable to native English speakers, while students whose first language is Spanish have only a 2 percent graduation rate (Gunderson, 2008).

Meeting the Needs of a Changing Population

Both the United States and Canada have a commitment to rights, freedoms, and opportunities with roots dating to the United States Constitution and Bill of Rights and to Canada's Constitution and Charter of Rights and Freedoms. Over the years, these rights and freedoms have been further defined by various laws, acts, regulations, and court rulings to include the right of English language learners to equal access to the curriculum, despite their lack of English proficiency.

Ensuring the Rights of English Language Learners in the United States

As early as 1974, the U.S. Supreme Court ruled in *Lau v. Nichols* that all students, including English language learners, must be given equal access to the core curriculum, that is, the set of courses required for graduation. Even so, English language learners frequently have been enrolled in low-level math classes in which the primary emphasis is on computation, ignoring the importance of language development in mathematics. Those enrolled in regular math classes have sometimes been left to struggle with little support for either language development or the development of meaningful mathematical understandings.

The No Child Left Behind Act of 2001 (NCLB) holds schools accountable for the academic performance of all students, including limited–English-speaking students. NCLB defines a student who qualifies for limited English proficient (LEP) services as an individual:

- Who was not born in the United States or whose native language is a language other than English

- Who is a Native American or Alaska Native, or a native resident of the outlying areas, and who comes from an environment where a language other than English has had a significant impact on the individual's level of English language proficiency

- Who is migratory, whose native language is a language other than English, and who comes from an environment where a language other than English is dominant

- Whose difficulties in speaking, reading, writing, or understanding the English language may be sufficient to deny the individual:

- The ability to meet the state's proficient level of achievement on state assessments
- The ability to successfully achieve in classrooms where the language of instruction is English
- The opportunity to participate fully in society (U.S. Department of Education, 2001)

Many English language learners also fall into other subgroups, including racial and ethnic groups, economically disadvantaged students, and special education programs, which often means the impact of these students' achievement levels is felt in two or three accountability groups. The result may be a greater impact of NCLB on schools with high subgroup populations (Capps, Fix, & Murray, 2005).

Under the No Child Left Behind Act, states may use up to six language proficiency levels, L1 (lowest) to L6, when reporting limited English proficiency data (U.S. Department of Education, 2001). The law does not specify the names of proficiency levels nor the tests used to determine them. The assessments must measure oral language, reading and writing skills, and under Title III, comprehension skills. Under Title III, school districts receive funds through state grants from the federal government to help "provide enhanced instructional opportunities" for immigrant and limited English proficient students (Department of Education, 2001).

In addition to assessments that measure language proficiency, NCLB requires that LEP students study the same content and pass the same content-area (math, reading, and, beginning in 2007–2008, science) assessments as other students, with appropriate accommodations, and that they be included in the data used to measure adequate yearly progress (AYP) (U.S. Department of Education, 2003). Some common accommodations include linguistic simplification, oral translation, reading assistance, bilingual dictionaries, and bilingual glossaries.

However, many states lack alternative assessments in each of the content areas as are required under NCLB due to the high cost of developing those assessments (Batt, Kim, & Sunderman, 2005).

Ensuring the Rights of English Language Learners in Canada

The Canadian Multiculturalism Act was enacted in July 1988. In its preamble, it summarizes Canada's history of commitment to the rights of its multicultural community. It reads, in part:

AND WHEREAS the Constitution of Canada recognizes the importance of preserving and enhancing the multicultural heritage of Canadians;

[. . .]

AND WHEREAS the *Official Languages Act* provide[s] that English and French are the official languages of Canada and neither abrogates nor derogates from any rights or privileges acquired or enjoyed with respect to any other language;

AND WHEREAS the *Citizenship Act* provides that all Canadians, whether by birth or by choice, enjoy equal status, are entitled to the same rights, powers and privileges and are subject to the same obligations, duties and liabilities;

AND WHEREAS the **Canadian Human Rights Act** provides that every individual should have an equal opportunity with other individuals to make the life that the individual is able and wishes to have [. . .];

AND WHEREAS Canada is a party to the **International Convention on the Elimination of All Forms of Racial Discrimination**, which Convention recognizes that all human beings are equal before the law [. . . Canada is a party] to the **International Covenant on Civil and Political Rights**, which Covenant provides that persons belonging to ethnic, religious or linguistic minorities shall not be denied the right to enjoy their own culture, to profess and practise their own religion or to use their own language;

AND WHEREAS the Government of Canada recognizes the diversity of Canadians as regards race, national or ethnic origin, colour and religion as a fundamental characteristic of Canadian society and is committed to a policy of multiculturalism designed to preserve and enhance the multicultural heritage of Canadians [. . .];

[. . .]

It is hereby declared to be the policy of the Government of Canada to [. . .] recognize and promote the understanding that multiculturalism reflects the cultural and racial diversity of Canadian society and acknowledges the freedom of all members of Canadian society to preserve, enhance and share their cultural heritage. (Canada Department of Justice, 1988)

Canada was the first nation to proclaim a multiculturalism act. As such, it was a patent acknowledgement that multiculturalism is an elemental feature of Canadian society, and language diversity is at the core of multiculturalism.

English Language Learners in Elementary and Secondary Schools in the United States

Several programs are designed to support limited English proficient students. *Bilingual education* refers to approaches in the classroom that use the primary languages of LEP students for instruction (National Association for Bilingual Education, 2006) and encompasses several programs that all provide at least some instruction in the student's primary language, including:

- Newcomer programs, which are short in duration and designed to help students acquire the basic English necessary to adapt to campus life

- Dual language programs, which to varying degrees provide instruction in both English and the native language

- Transitional bilingual programs, which use the foundation of the student's native language to transition him or her to the all-English mainstream courses of study

- Heritage language preservation programs, which provide education with the intent of preserving the student's language and culture, often used with student populations that speak an "endangered" language

Bilingual teachers are trained in second language acquisition theory and are bilingual, speaking English and the primary language of the second language learners whom they teach.

Although some states and districts opt to include bilingual education at the secondary level, most rely on English as a second language (ESL), sheltered instruction, and structured English immersion.

In most *English as a second language* secondary programs, students are pulled out of mainstream classes for part of the day to receive instruction in English as a second language. ESL teachers are certified educators trained in second language acquisition theory and generally focus on helping LEP students develop academic language proficiency. While ESL teachers generally provide content support, the shortage of ESL teachers with strong mathematics backgrounds often results in less support for mathematics than for other content areas.

Sheltered instruction, a term coined by Stephen Krashen (1985), is an approach used to teach language and content to English language learners. Academic subjects are taught in English using strategies that make content comprehensible to students and promote language development. Although the teacher may be ESL-certified, it is more likely he or she has received professional development in sheltered instruction strategies.

In *structured English immersion* programs, teachers conduct classroom conversations in English. Immersion is structured, planned, and intentionally provides a context for new language acquisition using visuals and manipulatives.

Unfortunately, many ELLs are placed in classes that are conducted solely in English without support for the student or the teacher, an approach that does not comply with the law.

The emphasis on testing frequently narrows the instructional focus to the content areas included on the standardized tests and may impact language programs offered to limited–English-speaking students, meaning that districts often increase the focus on rapid English acquisition (Capps, Fix, & Murray, 2005). As students are placed in content-area classes sooner and with greater frequency, and since mathematics is usually the first content-area class in which LEP students are mainstreamed, mathematics teachers are challenged to provide meaningful mathematics instruction to students who may lack the language skills to understand, participate, and communicate in classrooms where lecture is the primary mode of instruction.

English Language Learners in Elementary and Secondary Schools in Canada

Canada's system of education is much more federalist than that of the United States. Canada has no national Department of Education. Instead, each province and territory has its own Ministry of Education. (In some instances, there are two ministries, one for pre-elementary through secondary education and another for postsecondary education.) Development of the curriculum and its implementation and assessment rest primarily with the local district. There is, however, the

Council of Ministers of Education, Canada, formed in 1967, which provides a forum for the provincial and territorial ministers to meet to discuss and formulate action plans to address issues of common concern (Council of Ministers of Education, Canada, 2008). Among the most recent action by the council is the implementation of the Pan-Canadian Assessment Program (PCAP) in 2007, which measures student achievement in reading, mathematics, and science, in which a random sample of some twenty thousand students participated; however, the data have not been disaggregated to reflect the performance of language subgroups (Council of Ministers of Education, Canada, 2007).

Both elementary- and secondary-school immigrant students who enroll in Canadian schools are interviewed and evaluated by the local school to determine their level of language proficiency. Depending on the results of the evaluation, the student may be placed in a newcomer program for all or part of the school day. They receive language support in the areas of listening, speaking, reading, and writing, with teachers generally evaluating when the student is ready to participate in regular classes (He, 2008). Participation in provincial assessments varies, and the evaluation of whether the student has adequate knowledge to participate is generally left to the teacher and principal. Likewise, the decision to discontinue English as a second or foreign language services is inconsistent from district to district and across the country. According to the Coalition for Equal Access to Education (2009), the Canadian "federal government has not had any active role in developing a national strategy for ESL education for children and youth."

The Goal of *Making Math Accessible to English Language Learners*

Making Math Accessible to English Language Learners is written to provide practical classroom tips and suggestions to strengthen the quality of classroom instruction for teachers of mathematics in the United States and Canada. The tips and suggestions are based on research in practices and strategies that address the affective, linguistic, and cognitive needs of English language learners.

Although this resource centers on teaching English language learners, many of the tips and suggestions benefit all students. However, it is important to remember that while the tips and strategies we explore may benefit *all* learners, they are *necessary* for the acceleration of language and content acquisition by English language learners.

We will follow five case studies of composite student profiles throughout the book with opportunities for reflection to increase personal awareness of both the teacher's role and students' needs in the mathematics classroom, tasks to provide interaction with the content of the book, and hot tips for ideas applicable to real-world classroom situations. Sample responses to the reflections and tasks are provided in appendix C (page 143).

The first four chapters of *Making Math Accessible to English Language Learners* lay the foundation for working with ELLs in mathematics classrooms. In chapter 1, we will focus on the challenges facing teachers in their classrooms as they strive to ensure the success of English language learners. We will introduce the students in the case studies, whose needs will be a focus in each chapter. In chapter 2, we will look at affective supports, which show how a positive classroom environment enhances learning. Chapter 3 is designed to provide teachers with practical strategies and activities for supporting ELLs' language development while still teaching mathematics content. Chapter 4 centers on providing cognitive supports by teaching mathematics conceptually for long-term retention using a variety of practices, tools, and techniques.

Chapters 5 and 6 are designed to connect the fundamental supports outlined in chapters 1–4 with real-life classrooms. In chapter 5, we will use a lesson developed using the Five E (5E) instructional model, a teaching sequence that meets the needs of English language learners. The five phases of the sequence are:

1. **Engage**—The purpose is to pique students' interest, get them involved, and connect to their prior knowledge.

2. **Explore**—The purpose is to build understanding by allowing students to actively participate in exploring the concept.

3. **Explain**—The purpose is to formalize students' understanding of the concept at this point in the lesson. Communication among students and between the students and teacher is a key element of the phase.

4. **Elaborate**—The purpose is to extend or apply what students have learned to related concepts.

5. **Evaluate**—The purpose is for both students and the teacher to determine if the desired outcome (learning) has taken place.

In chapter 6, we will extend the lesson-planning process by adapting a traditional textbook lesson to the 5E instructional model. Finally, the appendices provide tools for teacher and student use, including a glossary of terms used in this resource.

The goal of *Making Math Accessible to English Language Learners* is to provide a useful tool for teachers to accelerate English language learners' acquisition of academic English and proficiency in meaningful mathematics.

It is not knowledge, but the act of learning, not possession but the act of getting there, which grants the greatest enjoyment. —Carl Gauss

The Challenges Facing English Language Learners and Their Teachers

Every student should have equitable and optimal opportunities to learn mathematics free from bias—intentional or unintentional—based on race, gender, socioeconomic status, or language. In order to close the achievement gap, all students need the opportunity to learn challenging mathematics from a well-qualified teacher who will make connections to the background, needs, and cultures of all learners.

—National Council of Teachers of Mathematics

Reflection 1.1

Choose one or more of the following questions, and respond in the margin. Write from your heart, your beliefs, and your past experience. Compare your answers to those on page 143.

- Why do some students transition to English very quickly while others attend English-speaking schools for many years without acquiring academic English?

- How can we make grade-level mathematics accessible to all students regardless of language proficiency?

- What are the best ways to help students who are not yet proficient in English experience meaningful mathematics?

- What skills do math teachers need to work with English language learners?

The rigorous mathematics set forth in the National Council of Teachers of Mathematics' (NCTM, 2000) *Principles and Standards for School Mathematics* and frequently reflected in state standards demands that educators rethink their teaching of mathematics to make the content accessible to linguistically diverse students. English language learners have traditionally performed at lower levels on standardized tests than other students, even other subgroups. Low language ability makes it difficult to measure mathematics achievement since the test measures language as well as content. Additionally, variables such as socioeconomic status, parent education, and family support may outweigh school influences in affecting student achievement.

According to Haynes (2003), the problem is compounded because many English language learners have gaps in their mathematics content background due to sporadic attendance or prior education under a curriculum vastly different from that in the United States and Canada. Consequently, ELLs get further and further behind their peers when they are denied the opportunity to solve meaningful mathematics and challenging problems because of language barriers.

Not only must ELLs learn the mathematics content, but they also must do so while learning vocabulary, the structure of the language, and mathematics discourse. Mathematics has its own register—language specific to mathematics—in which some words, such as *table* and *face*, have a meaning that is different from the meaning of the commonly used word. Combinations of common words sometimes form mathematical terms, such as *composite number, place value*, and *least common denominator*, in which the meaning of the combination of words is different from the sum of the separate definitions. Mathematics texts and word problems are conceptually packed, requiring vertical, horizontal, and sometimes diagonal reading. The student must adjust his or her reading speed to comprehend technical language containing symbols, which often means he or she must read the text or problem multiple times (Bye, 1975). However, just because a student is not proficient in English does not mean the student cannot think. Delaying English language learners' participation in true problem solving until they have mastered the English language is not an option. Listening, reading, speaking, and writing skills are the vehicles for understanding, participating in, and communicating mathematical concepts and skills—and must be taught concurrently with the mathematics (Crandall, Dale, Rhodes, & Spanos, 1985).

The Language Acquisition Process

In order to provide appropriate instruction to an English language learner that enables him or her to succeed in rigorous mathematics, it is helpful to understand the process of language acquisition.

According to Cummins (1981), without ELL instructional strategies, English language learners generally take four to seven years to become academically proficient in English. They usually go through a silent period of two to five months (Krashen, 1982) and spend the first couple of years learning Basic Interpersonal Communication Skills (BICS), which involves learning essential language skills from peers and television and in other informal settings. During this early stage of development, students require the use of concrete contexts in the classroom. If teachers do not use ELL instructional strategies, it often takes students another four to seven years to comfortably understand, process, and communicate using academic language and abstract concepts. Cummins (1981) coined the term *Cognitive Academic Language Proficiency* (CALP) to identify the ability to use academic language and abstract concepts. Figure 1.1 shows the journey of the English language learner toward abstract and academically challenging mathematics.

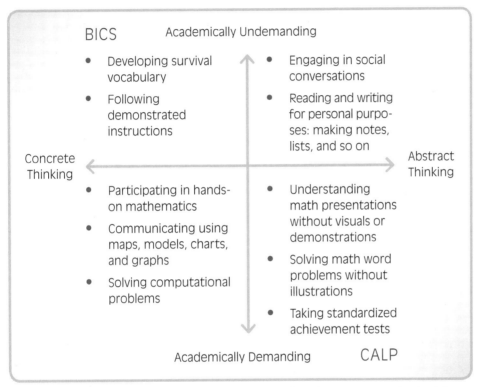

Figure 1.1: BICS and CALP in the mathematics classroom. (Adapted from Cummins, 1981.)

BICS are usually learned in *context-embedded* situations, such as talking with someone face-to-face or watching the teacher for nonverbal clues to receive immediate feedback. In contrast, CALP generally occurs in a *context-reduced* setting in which there are few clues to support comprehension. Students usually progress to an advanced level of academically undemanding English much more rapidly than to a level of demanding academic English. It is not unusual to encounter students who are quite proficient in social English while still performing at a very basic level in the language of mathematics (Cummins, 1981).

In order to accelerate students' progression from BICS to CALP, it is important to provide ongoing support in the classroom. In general, supports that are routine classroom practices are allowable in testing situations, whether the tests are teacher-made or standardized. (Check with your testing administrator for specific allowances.) These include:

- English and other language side-by-side tests

- Reading assistance
- Dictionaries
- Translation
- Bilingual glossaries
- English-language glossaries
- Simpler language
- Pictures and gestures

Determining Language Proficiency

When a student enrolls in a school, it is determined whether a language other than English is spoken at home. If so, the student's level of language proficiency must be determined. The student's language proficiency level may be determined through testing and/or observation. In the United States, the assessment criteria are generally determined by the state Department of Education. Under the No Child Left Behind Act, states may use up to six levels to describe the student's language proficiency. The proficiency levels used to describe the assessment results are shown in table 1.1; note that some states use more than one form of assessment.

Table 1.1: State Assessments Used to Determine Language Proficiency Levels

State	Assessment	Proficiency Levels
Alabama, Delaware, District of Columbia, Georgia, Illinois, Kentucky, Maine, New Hampshire, New Jersey, North Dakota, Oklahoma, Pennsylvania, Rhode Island, South Dakota, Vermont, Virginia, Wisconsin	Assessing Communication and Comprehension in English State to State for English Language Learners (ACCESS for ELLs)	- Entering - Beginning - Developing - Expanding - Bridging - Attained
Alaska, North Carolina, Utah	IDEA Proficiency Test (IPT)	- Beginner low - Beginner high - Intermediate low - Intermediate high - Proficient - Proficient high
Arizona, Mississippi	Stanford English Language Proficiency Test (SELP)	- Emergent - Basic - Intermediate - Proficient
Arkansas, Missouri	Maculaitis Assessment of Competencies Test of English Language Proficiency (MAC II)	- Prefunctional - Beginning - Intermediate - Advanced - Full English proficient

State	Assessment	Proficiency Levels
California	California English Language Development Test (CELDT)	• Beginning • Early intermediate • Intermediate • Early advanced • Advanced
Colorado	Colorado English Language Assessment	• Beginning • Early intermediate • Intermediate • Proficient • Advanced
Connecticut, Hawaii, Indiana, Maryland, Nevada	Language Assessment System Links (LAS)	• Beginner • Early intermediate • Intermediate • Advanced fluent • English proficient
Florida	Comprehensive English Language Learners Assessment (CELLA)	• Beginning • Low intermediate • High intermediate • Proficient
Idaho	Idaho English Language Assessments	• Beginning • Advanced beginning • Intermediate • Early fluent • Fluent
Iowa, Louisiana, Nebraska, Ohio, South Carolina, West Virginia	English Language Development Assessment (ELDA)	• Prefunctional • Beginner • Intermediate • Advanced • Fully English proficient
Kansas	Kansas English Language Proficiency Assessment	• Beginning • Intermediate • Advanced
Massachusetts	Massachusetts English Proficiency Assessment	• Beginning • Early intermediate • Intermediate • Transitioning
Michigan, Oregon	English Language Proficiency Assessment (ELPA)	• Basic • Low intermediate • High intermediate • Proficient
Minnesota	• Test of Emerging Academic English • Minnesota Student Oral Language Observation Matrix • Checklist for reading and writing for K–2 students	• Beginning • Intermediate • Advanced • Transitional

continued on next page→

State	Assessment	Proficiency Levels
Montana	• Iowa Test of Basic Skills • Woodcock-Muñoz Language Survey (English) • Other state-approved tests	• Negligible • Very limited • Limited • Fluent • Advanced
New Mexico	New Mexico English Language Proficiency Assessment (includes Mountain West Consortium test items)	• Beginning • Early intermediate • Intermediate • Early advanced • Advanced
New York	New York State English as a Second Language Achievement Test (NYSESLAT)	• Beginning • Intermediate • Advanced • English proficient
South Dakota	Dakota English Language Proficiency Assessment	• Emergent • Basic • Intermediate • Proficient
Tennessee	Comprehensive English Language Learners Assessment (CELLA)	• Beginner • High beginner • Intermediate • Advanced
Texas	Texas English Language Proficiency Assessment System (TELPAS)	• Beginning • Intermediate • Advanced • Advanced high
Washington	Washington Language Proficiency Test	• No English proficiency • Very limited English proficiency • Intermediate • Advanced
Wyoming	Wyoming English Language Learner Assessment	• Pre-emergent • Emergent • Basic • Intermediate • Proficient

Under Canada's educational system, districts tend to be more autonomous than in the United States; proficiency levels are most often determined via collaboration among the principal, teacher(s), and parent. The Canadian Language Benchmarks (CLB) are used to describe, measure, and recognize adult immigrants' language proficiency in speaking, listening, reading, and writing by using twelve levels within each descriptor, level 1 representing the most basic literacy level and level 8 roughly equivalent to that of a high school graduate. Levels 9–12 identify postsecondary language proficiency levels (Centre for Canadian Language Benchmarks, n.d.).

Schools frequently use the CLB levels as a guide to describe the language proficiency levels of English as a second or foreign language (ESL/EFL).

Proficiency Level Classifications

Since terms used to identify English language proficiency levels vary, the English language proficiency levels we will use that encompass the varied classifications are as follows:

- Beginning—This rating indicates the initial stages of learning English and minimal ability to communicate in English. Comprehension is demonstrated through action, gestures, and drawings.

- Early intermediate—This rating indicates the ability to use common, basic English in routine classroom activities. Comprehension is demonstrated through the use of key words and phrases and nonverbal responses.

- Intermediate—This rating indicates the ability to communicate more freely using some academic language. Comprehension is demonstrated using short phrases and sentences in context-embedded situations.

- Advanced—This rating indicates the ability to use academic English in classroom activities, using more complex phrases and sentences with English-language assistance provided when needed. Comprehension is demonstrated in context-reduced situations, both orally and in writing.

- Proficient—This rating indicates the ability to use academic English in classroom activities with the approximate fluency of non-ELL peers. Comprehension is demonstrated in situations with and without a context, both orally and in writing.

Table 1.2 (page 18) summarizes classroom indicators of English language proficiency levels.

Task: Identifying Language Proficiency Levels

Read each case study on pages 20–24, review each student's work, and use table 1.2 (page 18) to help you place the student according to English proficiency level by marking an *X* on the scale below each case study. After completing your work, compare your answers to those on page 143.

Table 1.2: Indicators of Levels of Student Proficiency

	Understanding	Participating	Communicating
Beginning	• Goes through a silent period of two to five months • Listens but responds in nonverbal ways • Finds math text incomprehensible with the exception of numerals and perhaps a few words linked to the student's background • Indicates understanding through facial expressions and body language • Can follow directions such as "Draw," "Circle," and action phrases such as "Line up" and "Move to your groups" when overtly demonstrated by the teacher	• Can actively participate in hands-on group activities • May "best guess" relationships among numbers in word problems based on past experience in the primary language • May mimic language without understanding what he or she is saying	• Speaks little, if any, English • Makes few language errors because attempts to speak English are limited
Early Intermediate	• Uses high-frequency nouns and present-tense verbs mixed with gestures when attempting to speak English • Uses basic, "simple" English • May procedurally solve math problems without understanding the concept	• May produce sentences by combining memorized words or phrases • May not seek clarification when does not understand	• Speaks and writes words and short phrases using basic vocabulary in routine situations • Generally listens more than speaks
Intermediate	• Solves simple word problems, but still has difficulty with multistep problems and problems at a high reading level, especially with a lengthy text • Can follow familiar social conversation	• Is more comfortable working with a partner or small group than in a whole-class setting • Can take a more active role in group activities • Begins to process simple problems independently	• Speaks and writes using short phrases and sentences • Makes language errors in pronunciation, grammar, and word order • Justifies answers with charts, graphs, tables, and drawings
Advanced	• May still have difficulty following conversations with pronouns • Understands high-frequency math words • May be confused by conditional structure of many word problems • Comprehends conversation	• Participates in social conversation without a great deal of contextual support • Functions moderately at an academic level • Develops increasing proficiency in solving word problems • Can assist other ELLs in cooperative groups • Can lead groups in activities • Comprehends conversation and can engage in student-to-teacher discourse	• Uses a wider range of vocabulary • Makes language errors less frequently and primarily of a complex nature, misusing or misinterpreting passive voice and conditional sentences • Can engage in student-to-student discourse • Justifies answers using complete sentences

	Understanding	Participating	Communicating
Proficient	• Has advanced cognitive skills and effectively understands grade-level academic language	• Participates in two-way conversations using academic English • Functions on grade level with peers	• Uses enriched vocabulary with few grammatical errors • May still find passive and conditional sentences difficult • Uses correct grammar, spelling, and formal mathematics vocabulary to justify answers • Has advanced cognitive skills and effectively uses academic language

Note: This chart is not a formal observation protocol. It is intended as an informal tool for the classroom teacher to approximate proficiency levels of English language learners.

Case Study: Anh

Anh and her parents are immigrants from Vietnam. Anh has many friends and attempts to converse with them in English but must watch closely for facial expressions and gestures to give her clues about what they are saying. Her computational skills in mathematics are excellent, but she is easily frustrated when trying to solve contextual problems.

How many different perimeters can a rectangle have if its area is equal to 24 square inches? Explain your thinking.

Area

Perimeter	Side	Side	Area
10	4	6	24
14	12	2	24
25	24	1	24
11	3	8	24

Answer: 8

Beginning   Early Intermediate   Intermediate   Advanced   Proficient

Case Study: Luca

Luca moved to Canada three years ago from Italy, where he attended a private school. He has an older brother in high school. Idioms and slang sometimes confuse Luca, but he communicates easily in descriptive English, readily learns concepts in his mathematics class, and communicates using appropriate academic language.

> How many different perimeters can a rectangle have if its area is equal to 24 square inches? Explain your thinking.
>
> If area = length x width, then 24 could be 1 x 24, 2 x 12, 4 x 6, or 3 x 8. If you make those numbers the sides, you get 1 + 1 + 24 + 24, 2 + 2 + 12 + 12, 4 + 4 + 6 + 6, 3 + 3 + 8 + 8. A rectangle with an area of 24 square inches can have 4 different perimeters. They are 50 inches, 28 inches, 20, and 22 inches.

Beginning   Early Intermediate   Intermediate   Advanced   Proficient

Case Study: Pakiza

Pakiza and her family recently emigrated from Pakistan. She is frequently absent from school and, when in class, relies on pictures, gestures, and translations by her bilingual friends for both understanding and communication.

> How many different perimeters can a rectangle have if its area is equal to 24 square inches? Explain your thinking.
>
> $$\begin{array}{r} 24 \\ \times\ 24 \\ \hline 96 \\ +\ 480 \\ \hline 576\ \text{inches} \end{array}$$

Beginning   Early Intermediate   Intermediate   Advanced   Proficient

Case Study: Camilo

Camilo and his mother came to the United States from Guatemala two years ago. He can read unmodified texts with occasional assistance. He converses easily in English, using some descriptive language. He can communicate ideas in mathematics class, especially when working with a cooperative group. Although he passed his mathematics and reading cumulative assessments, he did not pass the writing assessment.

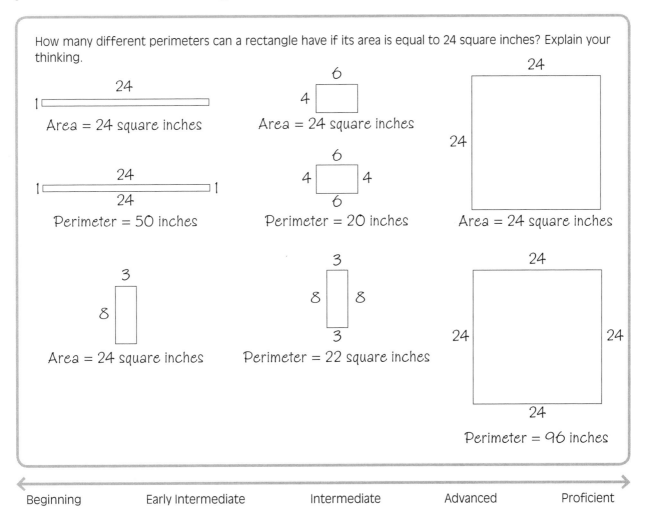

How many different perimeters can a rectangle have if its area is equal to 24 square inches? Explain your thinking.

Area = 24 square inches

Area = 24 square inches

Area = 24 square inches

Perimeter = 50 inches

Perimeter = 20 inches

Area = 24 square inches

Area = 24 square inches

Perimeter = 22 square inches

Perimeter = 96 inches

Beginning   Early Intermediate   Intermediate   Advanced   Proficient

Case Study: Lin

Fourteen months ago, Lin and his family left China and settled in Vancouver, where several of his relatives live. They provide encouragement and support to Lin and his parents. He relies on modified texts in reading and social studies and does well in math despite the unavailability of a modified text. He has difficulty with contextual problems but seeks help from his teacher and fellow students.

How many different perimeters can a rectangle have if its area is equal to 24 square inches? Explain your thinking.

1 x 24 = 24 area

Width = 1

Length =24

1 + 1 + 24 + 24 = 50 perimeter

2 x 12 = 24 area

Width = 2

Length = 12

2 + 2 + 12 + 12 = 28 perimeter

3 x 8 = 24 area

Length = 8

Width = 3

3 + 3 + 8 + 8 = 22 perimeter

4 x 6 = 24 area

Length = 6

Width = 4

4 + 4 + 6 + 6 = 20 perimeter

Beginning — Early Intermediate — Intermediate — Advanced — Proficient

As you will recall, it generally takes four to seven years for English language learners to achieve academic English fluency without ELL support (Cummins, 1981). There simply is not enough time between arrival as an English language learner and graduation to wait for students to become fluent in English before engaging them in rigorous mathematics. As Kessler (1985) expressed, our challenge as mathematics educators is to develop the student's mathematical proficiency while the student is still acquiring a second language—English.

Reflection 1.2

Using table 1.3, reflect on some of your present or former students who are English language learners. Compare your answers to those on page 144.

- Write the first name of a student next to the level that most accurately describes him or her. If possible, identify a student for each level.

- What do you think the student perceived as a particularly difficult challenge in your class?

- What was your greatest challenge as the student's teacher?

Table 1.3: Student Proficiency and Challenges

Language Proficiency	Student	Challenge for Student	Challenge for Teacher
Beginning			
Early Intermediate			
Intermediate			
Advanced			
Proficient			

BIG IDEAS

- English language learners are not required to be proficient in English prior to being placed in regular math classes.

- English language learners generally become proficient in social language much more rapidly than in academically demanding language.

- Students should be given opportunities to engage in rigorous mathematics, even though their English proficiency may be at a beginning level.

- By learning about the student's background and observing the student's work, the teacher can determine reasonable expectations and plan for appropriate understanding, participation, and communication strategies.

Points to Ponder

What will you do to learn more about your students' backgrounds?

Do you have high expectations for all your students?

What practices can you use to support your expectations?

Providing Affective Supports for English Language Learners

There are hundreds of languages in the world, but a smile speaks them all.
—Anonymous

> ### Reflection 2.1
> Imagine you are going to be an exchange student in a country where you do not know the language. What positive classroom aspects could motivate you to learn the language relatively quickly? Compare your answers to those on page 145.

The National Council of Teachers of Mathematics (2000) has articulated the importance of a positive classroom climate in learning mathematics. The classroom environment communicates subtle messages about what is valued in learning and doing mathematics and encourages students to participate in the learning and doing of mathematics. The English language learner's first impression of the classroom and the teacher sets the tone for learning and success. Putting yourself in the place of the student and envisioning what would make you feel welcome will put you on the right path toward creating a positive classroom climate that meets the needs of English language learners in learning mathematics.

A classroom that provides a warm and encouraging atmosphere meets what are called *affective needs,* which refers to students' feelings and emotions. An inviting classroom provides the opportunity for learning as well as a way to help students feel relaxed, emotionally safe, and at ease. When students do not understand, they will look around the classroom, so creating an attractive classroom with objects that are both informative and interesting will set the stage for learning.

HOT TIP!

We remember kindnesses shown to us. Create a memory for your students.

We all like to be called by our names and to have them pronounced correctly. Ask the student to say his or her name. Then repeat it back to the student. It is important to read the student's face to see if you said it correctly because many English language learners will hesitate to correct you since most cultures consider it rude to correct adults. To accelerate learning, face the class and use eye contact when speaking to the class so ELLs can use your facial expressions and watch your mouth as you form the words. When using an overhead projector or computer projection device, leave on some light so students can still watch your face and gestures for visual clues about what you are saying.

Using established routines will also accelerate learning. Students should know, for example, that they are to sharpen pencils before the bell rings and immediately have homework out to check and turn in while the teacher silently checks roll and returns homework from the previous day. Teaching routines such as saying "Raise your hand" and "Move to groups"—using the same words each time—empowers even beginning ELLs to quickly learn phrases that allow them to participate with more confidence. When students know what to expect each day, they feel safe and can learn efficiently. English language learners bring with them many strengths. Making opportunities for them to share and participate will benefit all students.

The most effective teachers provide subtle supports for English language learners, including being conscious of the physical setup of the classroom, developing an awareness of how they interact and share information with the students, and deciding how to provide opportunities for ELLs to get to know and work with non-ELLs. Table 2.1 outlines some strategies to use with all students, but particularly with English language learners.

> *Those who bring sunshine into the lives of others cannot keep it from themselves.*
>
> —James M. Barrie

Table 2.1: Affective Strategies to Support Understanding, Participating, and Communicating

Understanding	Participating	Communicating
• Smile. • Pronounce the student's name correctly. • Be sure the student knows your name. • Establish routines so students know what to expect. • Face the class when speaking. • Speak slowly and distinctly. • Avoid slang and explain idioms. • Write legibly. • Repeat important information. • Allow students to audio record lessons. • Label objects in the classroom, such as *trash* and *overhead projector*. • Create attractive, content-related bulletin boards. • Provide plenty of wait time. • Be patient, kind, understanding, and friendly. • Teach to appeal to all five senses.	• Smile. • Create a positive, nonthreatening classroom environment. • Create a nurturing environment. • Find opportunities to bring the student's culture and language into class. • Give frequent, genuine praise. • Establish routines so students know what to expect. • Post procedures and schedules. • Use flexible grouping. • Assign bilingual students as peer partners. • Have groups present work using chart paper and markers. • Highlight contributions of mathematicians from other cultures. • Be patient, kind, understanding, and friendly.	• Smile. • Be patient, kind, understanding, and friendly. • Provide plenty of wait time. • Create word walls. • Use personal response boards, which can be easily cut from bathroom tile-board. • Ask for thumbs up/thumbs down or other physical responses.

As table 2.1 notes, it is important to allow extra *wait time* for ELLs to respond to questions. While we understand that students at the lower levels of English proficiency need extra time to translate to their first language and then process the information before responding, it is not always apparent that even advanced and proficient students may need extra processing time. A colleague who immigrated at age thirteen has stated that to this day she cannot listen to a speaker and take notes at the same time. If she must take detailed notes, she records the lecture and then plays it back at a later time, listening and stopping the recording to write, then listening a bit more, and so on.

Flexible grouping is a powerful tool for increasing student learning. Speaking quietly to a group of students sitting together is far less intimidating for ELLs than addressing the entire class. *Heterogeneous grouping* allows ELLs to interact with non-ELLs in an environment that promotes collaboration and language development, whether students are randomly grouped or assigned to a group to complete a task or project based on similar interests. If there are several ELLs in the same class, the teacher sometimes may find it beneficial to *homogeneously group* students so that the teacher can work with the ELLs in a more intimate setting while other students work independently. Two important points to remember if group work is new to you: keep the groups small (no more than two or three students), and keep the duration short (less than ten minutes at first).

Students of any age like to color and display their work. *Chart paper* and *markers* are convenient, beneficial, and fun. Students can talk (quietly) as they produce their work, adding drawings or personal touches. When groups display their work, students have built-in opportunities to speak, using the chart-paper work as a prop. Students can also see whether their work "measures up" and collect ideas for future tasks. Additionally, the teacher benefits by being able to immediately correct any misconceptions.

Classroom walls seem to call out for some kind of covering. Why not put up something useful—beyond the bell schedule and lunch menu? *Word walls* are a visually appealing way to subtly teach vocabulary. Word walls are most effective when they include pictures or sketches and are arranged in such a way that students can use them to categorize the vocabulary in their minds. Later in this book we will look at vocabulary organizers, which can be used as student-generated elements of a word wall.

One of the easiest ways to be sure all students are actively involved in the lesson is with *personal response boards*. Students respond to questions or work problems on the response boards and, upon the teacher's signal, hold them up. Response boards automatically increase wait time because it is easier to know when everyone has finished. They allow nonverbal responses, and beginning ELLs can even make drawings to communicate. They also allow for all students, not just the ones with the quickest answers, to participate.

Manufactured whiteboards, often with lines or a coordinate grid on the reverse side, are handy, but homemade response boards can be made by cutting bathroom tileboard (shower board) into rectangles. Sheets of the tileboard can be found in building products stores. Even cheaper and easier, response boards can be made by slipping a sheet of card stock, which provides a bit of rigidity, into a clear plastic page protector, found at office supply stores. With any type of personal response board, the student will need a couple of dry erase markers in different colors and an old rag or sock to use as an eraser.

> ### Reflection 2.2
> Which of the affective practices in table 2.1 (page 28) do you use naturally? Which do you make a conscious effort to use? Which will you add to your repertoire? Compare your answers to those on page 145.

Task: Choosing Appropriate Affective Practices

We'll revisit the case studies from chapter 1 over the following pages. As you review them, thinking about the affective domain, which of the practices in table 2.1 would you use with each of the students in the case studies? Write your responses in the space provided. After completing your work, compare your answers to those on pages 145–146.

Case Study: Anh

Anh and her parents are immigrants from Vietnam. Anh has many friends and attempts to converse with them in English but must watch closely for facial expressions and gestures to give her clues about what they are saying. Her computational skills in mathematics are excellent, but she is easily frustrated when trying to solve contextual problems.

How many different perimeters can a rectangle have if its area is equal to 24 square inches? Explain your thinking.

Area

Perimeter	Side	Side	Area
10	4	6	24
14	12	2	24
25	24	1	24
11	3	8	24

Answer: 8

Beginning   Early Intermediate   Intermediate   Advanced   Proficient

Understanding	Participating	Communicating
☐ Smile. ☐ Pronounce the student's name correctly. ☐ Be sure the student knows your name. ☐ Establish routines so students know what to expect. ☐ Face the class when speaking. ☐ Speak slowly and distinctly. ☐ Avoid slang and explain idioms. ☐ Write legibly. ☐ Repeat important information. ☐ Allow students to audio record lessons. ☐ Label objects in the classroom, such as *trash* and *overhead projector.* ☐ Create attractive, content-related bulletin boards. ☐ Provide plenty of wait time. ☐ Be patient, kind, understanding, and friendly. ☐ Teach to appeal to all five senses.	☐ Smile. ☐ Create a positive, nonthreatening classroom environment. ☐ Create a nurturing environment. ☐ Find opportunities to bring the student's culture and language into class. ☐ Give frequent, genuine praise. ☐ Establish routines so students know what to expect. ☐ Post procedures and schedules. ☐ Use flexible grouping. ☐ Assign bilingual students as peer partners. ☐ Have groups present work using chart paper and markers. ☐ Highlight contributions of mathematicians from other cultures. ☐ Be patient, kind, understanding, and friendly.	☐ Smile. ☐ Be patient, kind, understanding, and friendly. ☐ Provide plenty of wait time. ☐ Create word walls. ☐ Use personal response boards, which can be easily cut from bathroom tileboard. ☐ Ask for thumbs up/thumbs down or other physical responses.

Case Study: Luca

Luca moved to Canada three years ago from Italy, where he attended a private school. He has an older brother in high school. Idioms and slang sometimes confuse Luca, but he communicates easily in descriptive English, readily learns concepts in his mathematics class, and communicates using appropriate academic language.

> How many different perimeters can a rectangle have if its area is equal to 24 square inches? Explain your thinking.
>
> If area = length x width, then 24 could be 1 x 24, 2 x 12, 4 x 6, or 3 x 8. If you make those numbers the sides, you get 1 + 1 + 24 + 24, 2 + 2 + 12 + 12, 4 + 4 + 6 + 6, 3 + 3 + 8 + 8. A rectangle with an area of 24 square inches can have 4 different perimeters. They are 50 inches, 28 inches, 20, and 22 inches.

Beginning   Early Intermediate   Intermediate   Advanced   Proficient

Understanding	Participating	Communicating
☐ Smile. ☐ Pronounce the student's name correctly. ☐ Be sure the student knows your name. ☐ Establish routines so students know what to expect. ☐ Face the class when speaking. ☐ Speak slowly and distinctly. ☐ Avoid slang and explain idioms. ☐ Write legibly. ☐ Repeat important information. ☐ Allow students to audio record lessons. ☐ Label objects in the classroom, such as *trash* and *overhead projector*. ☐ Create attractive, content-related bulletin boards. ☐ Provide plenty of wait time. ☐ Be patient, kind, understanding, and friendly. ☐ Teach to appeal to all five senses.	☐ Smile. ☐ Create a positive, nonthreatening classroom environment. ☐ Create a nurturing environment. ☐ Find opportunities to bring the student's culture and language into class. ☐ Give frequent, genuine praise. ☐ Establish routines so students know what to expect. ☐ Post procedures and schedules. ☐ Use flexible grouping. ☐ Assign bilingual students as peer partners. ☐ Have groups present work using chart paper and markers. ☐ Highlight contributions of mathematicians from other cultures. ☐ Be patient, kind, understanding, and friendly.	☐ Smile. ☐ Be patient, kind, understanding, and friendly. ☐ Provide plenty of wait time. ☐ Create word walls. ☐ Use personal response boards, which can be easily cut from bathroom tileboard. ☐ Ask for thumbs up/thumbs down or other physical responses.

Case Study: Pakiza

Pakiza and her family recently emigrated from Pakistan. She is frequently absent from school and, when in class, relies on pictures, gestures, and translations by her bilingual friends for both understanding and communication.

How many different perimeters can a rectangle have if its area is equal to 24 square inches? Explain your thinking.

$$\begin{array}{r} 24 \\ \times\ 24 \\ \hline 96 \\ +\ 480 \\ \hline 576\ \text{inches} \end{array}$$

Beginning   Early Intermediate   Intermediate   Advanced   Proficient

Understanding	Participating	Communicating
☐ Smile. ☐ Pronounce the student's name correctly. ☐ Be sure the student knows your name. ☐ Establish routines so students know what to expect. ☐ Face the class when speaking. ☐ Speak slowly and distinctly. ☐ Avoid slang and explain idioms. ☐ Write legibly. ☐ Repeat important information. ☐ Allow students to audio record lessons. ☐ Label objects in the classroom, such as *trash* and *overhead projector*. ☐ Create attractive, content-related bulletin boards. ☐ Provide plenty of wait time. ☐ Be patient, kind, understanding, and friendly. ☐ Teach to appeal to all five senses.	☐ Smile. ☐ Create a positive, nonthreatening classroom environment. ☐ Create a nurturing environment. ☐ Find opportunities to bring the student's culture and language into class. ☐ Give frequent, genuine praise. ☐ Establish routines so students know what to expect. ☐ Post procedures and schedules. ☐ Use flexible grouping. ☐ Assign bilingual students as peer partners. ☐ Have groups present work using chart paper and markers. ☐ Highlight contributions of mathematicians from other cultures. ☐ Be patient, kind, understanding, and friendly.	☐ Smile. ☐ Be patient, kind, understanding, and friendly. ☐ Provide plenty of wait time. ☐ Create word walls. ☐ Use personal response boards, which can be easily cut from bathroom tileboard. ☐ Ask for thumbs up/thumbs down or other physical responses.

Case Study: Camilo

Camilo and his mother came to the United States from Guatemala two years ago. He can read unmodified texts with occasional assistance. He converses easily in English, using some descriptive language. He can communicate ideas in mathematics class, especially when working with a cooperative group. Although he passed his mathematics and reading cumulative assessments, he did not pass the writing assessment.

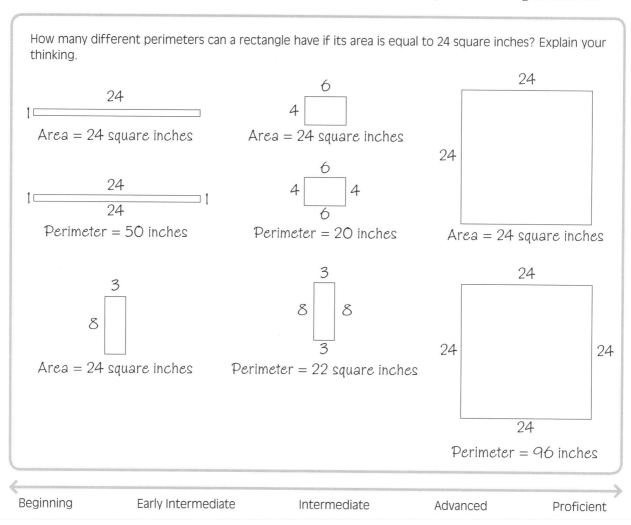

Understanding	Participating	Communicating
☐ Smile.	☐ Smile.	☐ Smile.
☐ Pronounce the student's name correctly.	☐ Create a positive, nonthreatening classroom environment.	☐ Be patient, kind, understanding, and friendly.
☐ Be sure the student knows your name.	☐ Create a nurturing environment.	☐ Provide plenty of wait time.
☐ Establish routines so students know what to expect.	☐ Find opportunities to bring the student's culture and language into class.	☐ Create word walls.
☐ Face the class when speaking.	☐ Give frequent, genuine praise.	☐ Use personal response boards, which can be easily cut from bathroom tileboard.
☐ Speak slowly and distinctly.	☐ Establish routines so students know what to expect.	
☐ Avoid slang and explain idioms.	☐ Post procedures and schedules.	
☐ Write legibly.	☐ Use flexible grouping.	
☐ Repeat important information.	☐ Assign bilingual students as peer partners.	☐ Ask for thumbs up/thumbs down or other physical responses.
☐ Allow students to audio record lessons.	☐ Have groups present work using chart paper and markers.	
☐ Label objects in the classroom, such as *trash* and *overhead projector*.	☐ Highlight contributions of mathematicians from other cultures.	
☐ Create attractive, content-related bulletin boards.	☐ Be patient, kind, understanding, and friendly.	
☐ Provide plenty of wait time.		
☐ Be patient, kind, understanding, and friendly.		
☐ Teach to appeal to all five senses.		

Case Study: Lin

Fourteen months ago, Lin and his family left China and settled in Vancouver, where several of his relatives live. They provide encouragement and support to Lin and his parents. He relies on modified texts in reading and social studies and does well in math despite the unavailability of a modified text. He has difficulty with contextual problems but seeks help from his teacher and fellow students.

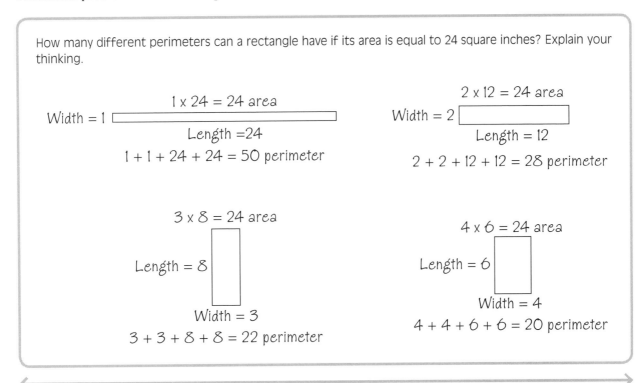

How many different perimeters can a rectangle have if its area is equal to 24 square inches? Explain your thinking.

Width = 1 $1 \times 24 = 24$ area
Length =24
$1 + 1 + 24 + 24 = 50$ perimeter

Width = 2 $2 \times 12 = 24$ area
Length = 12
$2 + 2 + 12 + 12 = 28$ perimeter

$3 \times 8 = 24$ area
Length = 8
Width = 3
$3 + 3 + 8 + 8 = 22$ perimeter

$4 \times 6 = 24$ area
Length = 6
Width = 4
$4 + 4 + 6 + 6 = 20$ perimeter

Beginning — Early Intermediate — Intermediate — Advanced — Proficient

Understanding	Participating	Communicating
☐ Smile. ☐ Pronounce the student's name correctly. ☐ Be sure the student knows your name. ☐ Establish routines so students know what to expect. ☐ Face the class when speaking. ☐ Speak slowly and distinctly. ☐ Avoid slang and explain idioms. ☐ Write legibly. ☐ Repeat important information. ☐ Allow students to audio record lessons. ☐ Label objects in the classroom, such as *trash* and *overhead projector*. ☐ Create attractive, content-related bulletin boards. ☐ Provide plenty of wait time. ☐ Be patient, kind, understanding, and friendly. ☐ Teach to appeal to all five senses.	☐ Smile. ☐ Create a positive, nonthreatening classroom environment. ☐ Create a nurturing environment. ☐ Find opportunities to bring the student's culture and language into class. ☐ Give frequent, genuine praise. ☐ Establish routines so students know what to expect. ☐ Post procedures and schedules. ☐ Use flexible grouping. ☐ Assign bilingual students as peer partners. ☐ Have groups present work using chart paper and markers. ☐ Highlight contributions of mathematicians from other cultures. ☐ Be patient, kind, understanding, and friendly.	☐ Smile. ☐ Be patient, kind, understanding, and friendly. ☐ Provide plenty of wait time. ☐ Create word walls. ☐ Use personal response boards, which can be easily cut from bathroom tileboard. ☐ Ask for thumbs up/thumbs down or other physical responses.

Factors Affecting Second Language Acquisition

According to Echevarria, Vogt, and Short (2004), how quickly an English language learner becomes proficient in English and mathematics is influenced by many factors, including:

- Motivation
- Age
- Access to the language
- Personality
- First language development
- Cognitive ability
- Effective instruction

Let's examine each of these factors.

Motivation

The degree to which a student has a desire or a sense of urgency to learn the language is an important factor in determining his or her rate of language acquisition. The family's priorities concerning language, learning, and education influence the student's desire to become language and content proficient. When there is a large community that speaks the primary language, parents and their children may see little practical need to acquire English. Teachers, counselors, and student mentors can provide opportunities for students to understand the doors that open to those who are fluent in English.

Age

Children who learn a language at a very young age are able to do so naturally and with great ease and efficiency. When the English language learner begins learning English when he or she is already in school, the student generally must learn both oral and written language simultaneously. However, the older ELL may use his or her advanced cognitive abilities to an advantage with formal language instruction. Labeling objects, establishing routines, and allowing students to work with a partner or small group can aid them in transitioning to classroom life quickly.

Access to the Language

When a language other than English is spoken at home and among friends, the *contact hours* in English are reduced, meaning the student has less opportunity to practice the language. If students are also removed from the opportunity to interact with other students in class, the problem is compounded. Encourage students to associate with each other outside the classroom as well as in cooperative groups.

> ### Reflection 2.3
> Imagine you are going to be an exchange teacher in Austria for a year. What advantages do you have in learning the German language? Write your answers in the margin, and compare them to those on page 146.

Personality

Many students have a fairly large receptive vocabulary but are limited in their ability to converse because they lack practice. Extroverts make friends and interact with classmates easily, while introverts often remain alone unless drawn out by others. Those tendencies directly affect language acquisition. Teachers can provide venues for conversation by providing opportunities for students to work with a partner or small group.

First Language Development

Some English language learners have not had the opportunity to become proficient in their primary language. They may not have been enrolled in any school for months or possibly years. They may have attended school only sporadically and may not have learned to read or write on grade level. Their exposure to the content areas may be limited. In some countries, mathematics is still taught procedurally and involves little contextual problem solving. Students may enter classrooms able to compute well but with little conceptual understanding of mathematics, or with conceptual understanding but weak computation skills.

Cognitive Ability

Students come to us with varying levels of cognitive ability. It is the charge of all educators to reach all students effectively, regardless of the ability of the student. On one hand, English language learners may be placed in special education because learning disabilities are often confused with language deficiencies. On the other hand, ELLs with learning disabilities may not be identified because the learning disability may be dismissed as a language deficiency. English language learners with learning disabilities can still learn a second language although their proficiency levels will be equal to or less than their primary language proficiency.

Effective Instruction

Effective instruction in both language and content is a major factor in accelerating the student's proficiency. Krashen (1982) asserts that providing comprehensible input through a *low affective filter* is the most important variable in helping students become proficient in both language and content. An affective filter such as nervousness or fear blocks or decreases student learning because it is more difficult for students to learn when they are nervous, afraid, or anxious. By creating a *low* affective filter, teachers set the stage for increased language and content learning. Effective instruction is evident when students are participating, when information is clearly communicated, and when students' understanding can be seen in their work.

Task: Aligning Affective Practices to Second Language Acquisition Factors

Refer to table 2.2. Starting with the first practice, "Smile," place a check under each language acquisition factor (such as motivation or age) that could be influenced by that practice. For example, while a smile might affect motivation, it cannot influence age. A smile might have a very small effect on personality, but it will not have an impact on access to language, first language development, or cognitive ability. A smile can, however, impact the effectiveness of instruction. Continue to place checks to indicate your responses for each practice. After completing your work, compare your answers to those on page 147.

Table 2.2: Affective Practices for Specific Second Language Acquisition Factors

Practice	Motivation	Age	Access to the Language	Personality	First Language Development	Cognitive Ability	Effective Instruction
Smile.							
Pronounce the student's name correctly.							
Be sure the student knows your name.							
Establish routines so students know what to expect.							
Face the class when speaking.							
Speak slowly and distinctly.							
Avoid slang and explain idioms.							
Write legibly.							
Repeat important information.							
Allow students to audio record lessons.							
Label objects in the classroom, such as *trash* and *overhead projector*.							
Create attractive, content-related bulletin boards.							
Provide plenty of wait time.							
Be patient, kind, understanding, and friendly.							
Teach to appeal to all five senses.							

Practice	Motivation	Age	Access to the Language	Personality	First Language Development	Cognitive Ability	Effective Instruction
Create a positive, nonthreatening classroom environment.							
Create a nurturing environment.							
Find opportunities to bring the student's culture and language into class.							
Give frequent, genuine praise.							
Post procedures and schedules.							
Use flexible grouping.							
Assign bilingual students as peer partners.							
Have groups present work using chart paper and markers.							
Highlight contributions of mathematicians from other cultures.							
Create word walls.							
Use personal response boards, which can be easily cut from bathroom tile board.							
Ask for thumbs up/thumbs down or other physical responses.							

Reflection 2.4

Over which of the affective factors do you have no influence? Over which of the factors do you have some influence? Over which of the factors do you have the greatest influence? Compare your answers to those on page 148.

Children are like wet cement. Whatever falls on them makes an impression.

—Haim Ginott

BIG IDEAS

- English language learners benefit from a classroom environment that encourages understanding, participating, and communicating.
- Use practices that instill confidence, build self-assurance, and demonstrate respect for heritage.
- Some of the factors that influence second language acquisition are:
  - Motivation
  - Age
  - Access to the language
  - Personality
  - First language development
  - Cognitive ability
  - Effective instruction
- Providing quality classroom interaction is the factor most within teacher control.

Points to Ponder

What affective supports are available for English language learners in your school?

What new affective supports can you use to enhance the effectiveness of instruction?

Providing Linguistic Supports for English Language Learners

Mathematics knows no race or geographic boundaries; for mathematics, the cultural world is one country.   —David Hilbert

The following example in figure 3.1 is what a student at the *beginning* level of language proficiency might read and comprehend. The blanks indicate words that the student likely would not be able to read or understand. Take a moment to try to solve the problem, thinking about what you can determine from the information given. Then do the same with the problem for each level that follows.

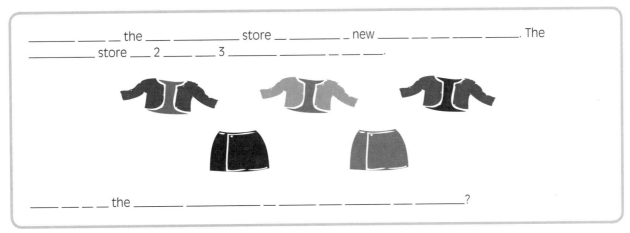

Figure 3.1: Comprehension at beginning proficiency.

A bit frustrating, isn't it? You can probably decipher only a few words and pick out the numbers. Even if the student has the mathematics background in his or her primary language, he or she cannot determine enough information to solve the problem.

41

Figure 3.2 shows what an English language learner at the *early intermediate* level of language proficiency might read and comprehend.

Candace _____ __ the ____ _____ store __ _____ a new _____ __ her piano _____. The _____ store ___ 2 skirts and 3 sweaters _____ _ her ___.

What ___ all __ the different _____ __ _____ ____ Candace ___ _____?

Figure 3.2: Comprehension at early intermediate proficiency.

Students at the early intermediate level are beginning to learn some social vocabulary and the structure of the English language but still struggle with comparatives, verb tenses, and vocabulary—especially academic vocabulary.

Figure 3.3 shows what a student at the *intermediate* level of language proficiency might read and comprehend.

Candace went __ the ____ department store __ _____ a new _____ __ her piano _____. The department store ___ 2 skirts and 3 sweaters _____ in her ___.

What are all __ the different _____ __ _____ that Candace can _____?

Figure 3.3: Comprehension at intermediate proficiency.

Even though students at the intermediate level have likely acquired an active social vocabulary, they may not possess the mathematics vocabulary or understanding of the abstract structure of the language in mathematical problems such as the one in figure 3.3 to reach the solution without significant support. Students at the intermediate level still struggle with prepositions and the conditional structure of mathematics text.

Figure 3.4 shows what a student at the *advanced* level of language proficiency might read and comprehend.

Candace went to the local department store to purchase a new outfit ___ her piano _____. The department store had 2 skirts and 3 sweaters _____ in her size.

What are all of the different _____ of outfits that Candace can purchase?

Figure 3.4: Comprehension at advanced proficiency.

At the advanced level, students are proficient enough in both English and the language of mathematics to solve the problem with some ELL support; they may continue to have difficulty with prepositions that do not indicate position, pronouns, conditional sentences, passive voice, and words with different common and mathematical meanings (such as *table*). An example of a conditional sentence is:

- *If* Johnny has one penny one day and doubles that amount each day thereafter, how much money *would* he have on the thirty-first day?

An example of active voice versus passive voice is as follows:

- Active voice—Johnny hit the ball.
- Passive voice—The ball was hit by Johnny.

Students may frequently struggle with reversals between English and number expressions: *three less than five* should be written 5 – 3, but ELLs may write 3 – 5 instead.

We would expect students at the *proficient* level to read problems on grade level with few, if any, LEP modifications. Figure 3.5 shows the original problem.

Candace went to the local department store to purchase a new outfit for her piano recital. The department store had 2 skirts and 3 sweaters available in her size.

What are all of the different combinations of outfits that Candace can purchase?

Figure 3.5: Comprehension at English proficiency.

Linguistic Obstacles

To observe a student in conversation with other students does not necessarily indicate he or she is fluent in academic English (Cummins, 1981). Being proficient in social situations is very different from being fluent in the language of mathematics. Look for clues by comparing written work, spoken responses, and conversational language. Even when students are at the advanced level of proficiency in the language of mathematics and the content of the course, the number of steps required to solve problems may pose a challenge. The length of the text is also a factor in students' persistence. If the text is too long, they will likely give up.

Common meanings for words such as *product* (something produced by labor or the result of a multiplication computation), *sum* (or *some*), or *base* (baseball base or bottom face of a geometric figure) may confuse ELLs in mathematical contexts. Although a student may know *product* in his or her primary language, he or she may not be able to use the word unless the vocabulary is actively taught, defined in a modified text, or discovered while participating in activities.

Authors of mathematics texts generally write in a very terse or compact style. Each sentence contains a large amount of compressed information with little redundancy. Unlike reading a story, when solving math problems, students find it difficult to determine meaning by using the surrounding context. Instead, they must construct meaning by making connections between the new information and their prior knowledge about the topic. The stronger and more varied the background a reader has in terms of knowledge and skills, the faster he or she will learn and be able to apply what he or she reads (Barton & Heidema, 2002).

> ## Is Reading Math Hard?
>
> Janey bought *some products* to use in her hair with a *sum* value of $12. The *products* should last a month. Since they were on sale, she decided to buy enough to last a year. What number would she multiply by to find the *product* of the *products?*
>
> A company builds *tables* with tops of increasing sizes so the *tables* nest. Create a *table* to represent the measurements of the *tables.*

The examples in figure 3.6 reveal the knowledge and skills not taught in other content areas that are required to read mathematics. Students must be able to read left to right, right to left, top to bottom, and bottom to top (see examples 1 and 2). They must be proficient at decoding not only words, but also numeric and non-numeric symbols and graphics (see example 3).

Use of technical terminology and abstractions, words with different meanings in everyday language and mathematics, and synonyms pose additional challenges for English language learners and their math teachers. Think about the difficulties an ELL might have with the words *series, figures, pattern,* and *square* (see example 4).

Example 1

The table below shows the total amount of money that Jacklynn will make from selling different numbers of rolls of wrapping paper.

Number of Rolls of Wrapping Paper	Total Amount of Money Made
2	$14
3	$21
5	$35
8	$56

If Jacklynn sells 11 rolls of wrapping paper, how much money will Jacklynn make?

Answer: $77

Example 2

Use the table to record the coordinates of the 4 points shown on the graph.

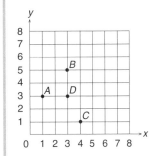

Point	Coordinates
A	(1, 3)
B	(3, 5)
C	(4, 1)
D	(3, 3)

Example 3

Which two line segments shown here are parallel to each other?

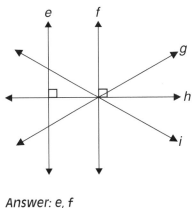

Answer: e, f

Example 4

Tobin created a series of figures whose areas created a pattern. If the pattern continues, what could be the length and width of figure 5?

Figure	1	2	3	4
Length (inches)	3	5	9	5
Width (inches)	5	6	5	12
Area (square inches)				

Answer: See table 3.1, page 46, for a possible solution.

Figure 3.6: Sample math problems.

Concepts are frequently embedded in other concepts (Barton & Heidema, 2002). In example 4, for students to understand conceptually how to find the length and width of the fifth figure, they must understand the relationship between length and width and the resulting area. Only by finding the pattern in the areas of the first four figures can they determined the length and width of the fifth figure in the pattern (see table 3.1, page 46).

Since the area of the fifth figure must be 75 square inches, one possible solution is a length of 15 inches and a width of 5 inches. The length and width measures could be reversed. Another possible whole-number solution is a length of 25 inches and a width of 3 inches. Problems with multiple possible solutions present challenges for all students, not just English language learners.

Table 3.1: Sample Solve of Example 4

Figure	1	2	3	4	5
Length (inches)	3	5	9	5	15
Width (inches)	5	6	5	12	5
Area (square inches)	15	30	45	60	75

Task: Determining Linguistic Obstacles

Review the examples of what beginning, early intermediate, intermediate, and advanced students might read and comprehend about the clothing problem, and compare those examples to the full original problem. In the space provided, note features of the problem that make it difficult to decode for students at each level of language proficiency. After completing your work, compare your answers to those on page 148.

Candace went to the local department store to purchase a new outfit for her piano recital. The department store had 2 skirts and 3 sweaters available in her size.

What are all of the different combinations of outfits that Candace can purchase?

Comprehension at English proficiency.

_____ ____ __ the ____ _____ store __ _____ __ new ____ __ __ ____ _____. The _____ store ___ 2 _____ ___ 3 _____ _____ __ ___ ___.

_____ __ _ __ the _____ _____ __ _____ ___ _____ __ _____?

Comprehension at beginning proficiency.

Candace _____ __ the _____ _____ store __ _____ a new _____ __ her piano _____. The _____ store ___ 2 skirts and 3 sweaters _____ _ her ___.

What ___ all __ the different _____ __ _____ ___ Candace ___ _____?

Comprehension at early intermediate proficiency.

Candace went __ the _____ department store __ _____ a new _____ __ her piano _____. The department store ___ 2 skirts and 3 sweaters _____ in her ___.

What are all __ the different _____ __ _____ that Candace can _____?

Comprehension at intermediate proficiency.

Candace went to the local department store to purchase a new outfit ___ her piano _____. The department store had 2 skirts and 3 sweaters _____ in her size.

What are all of the different _____ of outfits that Candace can purchase?

Comprehension at advanced proficiency.

Overcoming Linguistic Obstacles

If students are to become fluent in the language of mathematics, teachers must guide and support the reading process (Barton & Heidema, 2002). They must equip students with strategies to understand mathematical text at the same time the students are learning math concepts.

Provide Opportunities for Nonverbal Communication

As we have discussed, beginning English language learners usually go through a silent period (Krashen, 1982). Teachers who make the effort to provide opportunities for nonverbal communication will be rewarded with students who quickly progress beyond this silent period. Picture dictionaries, bilingual dictionaries, audio recorders, and videos are valuable classroom resources that encourage ELLs to support their own learning of English. Picture dictionaries and bilingual dictionaries foster independence since the ELL can find meanings of words and concepts without having to ask the teacher or another student, and audio recordings and videos let the student replay lessons as many times as necessary.

Preview Lesson Vocabulary and Content

Another option for beginning, early intermediate, and intermediate students is the *lesson preview*, in which the content teacher, ESL or bilingual teacher, or

Education, beyond all other devices of human origin, is the great equalizer of the conditions of man, the balance-wheel of the social machinery.

—Horace Mann

paraprofessional provides the student with a summary of the lesson. The 5E model enables students to acquire the math vocabulary; however, preteaching general vocabulary and providing a lesson summary will give the student more equal footing as the lesson is taught. This summary is not a translation. If a teacher or paraprofessional translates the lesson, the student will quickly learn to tune out the English and rely on the translation. Working with the ESL teacher to preview general vocabulary and, if possible, math content, provides an additional opportunity for language and content practice—as well as the opportunity to learn from a teacher who may provide a different approach to learning.

Reading and language arts teachers can also help by incorporating essential non-math vocabulary into their lessons; many are eager to help students develop the different meanings of words in nonacademic and nonmathematical contexts.

Provide Linguistic Supports

Continued progress is dependent on teachers providing supports appropriate to the student's proficiency level. If English language learners are to have the same opportunities to succeed as their peers, they must acquire English language and mathematics proficiency simultaneously. Notice in table 3.2 (pages 50–52), that promoting understanding, participating, and communicating in ELLs requires teachers to support learning of both general English and the specialized language of mathematics. You may also notice that some of the strategies in table 3.2 were also included as affective supports. It is not unusual for strategies to support English language learners in more than one domain.

> ### Reflection 3.1
>
> Using table 3.2 (pages 50–52), check the box for each practice you already use. Review the remaining practices, and choose one or more practices you think would be effective to use with your ELL students. Responses will vary.
>
> 1. Why did you select the practice or practices?
> 2. What can you do to incorporate the practice or practices in your classroom?
> 3. What is a challenge you may encounter in implementing the practice or practices, and how might you overcome the challenge?

You can use the linguistic strategies on a daily basis to enhance the learning experience of students. In your efforts to increase students' knowledge and background for continued studies in mathematics, be sure to consider the students' *prior* knowledge and background as well. Prior knowledge and background affect how easily students acquire new knowledge and skills. In addition, prior knowledge must also be accessible in long-term memory. When teachers help students learn to organize similar concepts and terminology and facilitate their understanding of the relationship between them, the information becomes accessible in long-term memory (Barton & Heidema, 2002). Learning has occurred when students can retrieve new knowledge from long-term memory.

Table 3.2: Linguistic Strategies to Support Understanding, Participating, and Communicating

Proficiency Level	Understanding	Participating	Communicating
Beginning	☐ Let your body language and the tone of your voice show students you enjoy teaching. ☐ Speak slowly. (Speaking louder does not help students understand.) ☐ Simplify your vocabulary. ☐ Enunciate clearly. Avoid *gonna, gotta,* and *lotsa.* ☐ Avoid slang and idioms. ☐ Demonstrate what you are talking about with your hands and other gestures. ☐ Use pictures and sketches for clarification. ☐ Write legibly. ☐ Write in print, which is easier to read than cursive. ☐ Use sans-serif fonts such as Arial (instead of serif fonts such as Times New Roman).	☐ Create a learning center or section on a bookshelf that might include: 　• Picture dictionary 　• Illustrated math dictionary 　• Bilingual dictionary 　• Native language textbook ☐ Have student groups produce collaborative work to share with other groups and/or the class. ☐ If possible, pair new arrivals with a bilingual student or aide. ☐ Incorporate manipulatives and real-life objects into lessons. ☐ Provide activities that allow the student to draw, match, circle, choose, point, or act out. ☐ If possible, provide translations of textbooks and assignments.	☐ Learn to read students' expressions for clues to determine whether they understand. ☐ Provide opportunities for the student to respond by drawing, matching, circling, choosing, pointing, acting, and demonstrating. ☐ Accept visual representations such as charts, graphs, and drawings.
Early Intermediate	*Continue to use the strategies listed above as needed, and:* ☐ Emphasize nouns and verbs with your voice while speaking. ☐ Repeat frequently, using the same phrases and sentences to allow students time to translate. ☐ Provide wait time. Remember, it takes longer to process in a second language. ☐ Teach content vocabulary using word matches, with cognates if appropriate. ☐ Provide sentence starters. ☐ Provide word banks with activities and for sentence starters. ☐ Encourage students to speak and write using complete sentences to reinforce learning the structure of the English language. ☐ Provide partially completed notes with sketches. ☐ Post key vocabulary. ☐ If the resources are available, provide lesson previews.	*Continue to use the strategies listed above as needed, and:* ☐ Have ELLs work with a partner or in small groups of students, including students who are not ELLs. ☐ Design lessons that relate to the students' backgrounds and prior knowledge. ☐ Tie lessons to students' interests. ☐ Provide activities that allow students to list, label, identify, and answer in short strings of words. ☐ Allow ELLs to audio record lessons and replay as needed to help with assignments. ☐ Simplify the language and highlight important words on assignments.	*Continue to use the strategies listed above as needed, and:* ☐ Structure questions that allow the students to respond in a way appropriate to their proficiency.

Proficiency Level	Understanding	Participating	Communicating
Intermediate	*Continue to use the strategies listed above as needed, and:* ☐ Encourage output. Speaking and writing are evidence that the student has understood what he or she heard or read. ☐ Encourage ELLs to use illustrated mathematics dictionaries. ☐ Teach special mathematics meanings for words commonly used in English (such as *point, base, and lateral*). ☐ Rewrite word problems in simpler language, using illustrations when possible. ☐ Teach content vocabulary using word matches. ☐ Reinforce vocabulary by having students create vocabulary organizers. ☐ Summarize learning by having students create concept definition maps. ☐ Teach comparison words: *more, less, most, least, greater than, equal, half as much, twice as many.* ☐ Teach mathematics vocabulary using tools such as vocabulary concept definition maps and word walls. ☐ Have students prepare their own glossaries of mathematical terms.	*Continue to use the strategies listed above as needed, and:* ☐ Provide opportunities for students to respond by listing, labeling, identifying, and answering in short strings of words.	*Continue to use the strategies listed above as needed, and:* ☐ Encourage students to use student-generated glossaries and word banks. ☐ Do not penalize students for mistakes in grammar and pronunciation. ☐ Be sensitive when correcting errors in grammar and pronunciation.
Advanced	*Continue to use the strategies listed above as needed, and:* ☐ Continue to use ELL-adapted materials as needed. ☐ Provide accommodations on assessments as needed.	*Continue to use the strategies listed above as needed, and:* ☐ Provide opportunities for student-to-teacher and student-to-student dialogue in which more complex language is required. ☐ Provide opportunities for students to describe, define, explain, compare, contrast, and justify.	*Continue to use the strategies listed above as needed, and:* ☐ Encourage students to write using complex sentences with more academic language. ☐ Use journals. ☐ Provide opportunities for students to speak using longer and more complex phrases and sentences. ☐ Provide opportunities for students to respond by describing, defining, explaining, comparing and contrasting, and justifying.

continued on next page →

Proficiency Level	Understanding	Participating	Communicating
Proficient	*Continue to use the strategies listed above as needed, and:* ☐ Provide opportunities to work with more complex text. ☐ Provide opportunities for understanding differences in intonations in English. (For instance, statements, questions, and exclamations all have different inflections.)	*Continue to use the strategies listed above as needed, and:* ☐ Provide opportunities for leadership to encourage language output. ☐ Design activities that require higher levels of language and mathematics.	*Continue to use the strategies listed above as needed, and:* ☐ Expect students to write complex sentences using correct grammar, spelling, and academic language. ☐ Expect students to demonstrate well-developed metacognitive skills (the ability to think about one's own thinking process).

Build Vocabulary

Graphic representations enhance student memory. In fact, *graphic organizers* are more effective learning tools for mathematics concepts than colorful pictures and photographs (Imhof et al., 1996, cited in Barton & Heidema, 2002). One of the most commonly used graphic organizers is a *semantic map*, which is usually used during the Engage phase of a lesson to activate prior knowledge and help students visualize connections among concepts (Barton & Heidema, 2002). A second commonly used graphic organizer is the *concept definition map*, which is usually used after students have completed an activity. It gives students an organized way in which to demonstrate their learning and the connections among the lesson or unit concepts (Schwartz, 1998, cited in Barton & Heidema, 2002).

Another graphic representation that relies heavily on the use of visual representations and connections to students' backgrounds is a *vocabulary organizer.* The personal association can be a sketch, real-world example, or translation of the term to the student's primary language. The purpose is to provide a connection to the student's background and prior knowledge.

Figure 3.7 is a combination of the Frayer model (Frayer, Frederick, & Klausmeier, 1969, cited in Barton & Heidema, 2002) and the Verbal and Visual Word Association (Readence, Bean, & Baldwin, 2001, cited in Barton & Heidema, 2002) strategies. Including examples and nonexamples is critical because they are often the most obvious indicator of any student misconceptions.

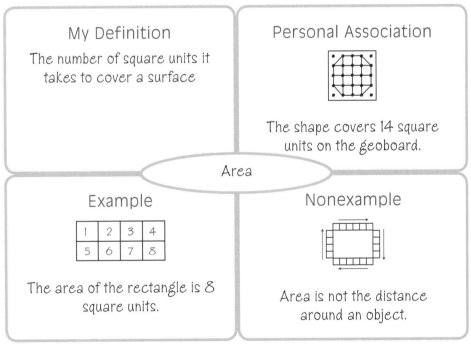

Figure 3.7: Sample vocabulary organizer.

Use Think-Alouds

It is important to introduce graphic organizers with teacher *think-alouds*. The teacher verbalizes his or her thought process in developing the concept definition map, vocabulary organizer, or problem solution (Davey, 1983). When students first begin using a vocabulary concept definition map, they will need help in choosing meaningful mathematical examples and nonexamples. For instance, drawing a tree would not be an appropriate nonexample in the vocabulary organizer shown in figure 3.7 (page 53) since a tree has no meaningful characteristics related to the area. A meaningful nonexample possesses characteristics that can be compared to and contrasted with the term or concept being developed. In the nonexample in figure 3.7, it is clear the student understands the area is not the distance around an object.

After the think-aloud, groups of students can begin developing their own concept definition maps, vocabulary organizers, or problem solutions in their groups, with the teacher facilitating. Posting work provides the opportunity for students to examine other groups' efforts and enrich their thinking. Working together as a group and sharing the work product allows English language learners the opportunity to actively participate in learning vocabulary and concepts.

HOT TIP!

Prompt groups to create concept definition maps and/or vocabulary organizers on chart paper to post as a word wall.

Task: Creating a Vocabulary Organizer

Decide on a mathematics vocabulary word, and use the vocabulary organizer in figure 3.8 to develop it. Have students begin a new vocabulary organizer when a concept is introduced. Then, as the concept is developed, they can add more details.

My Definition	Personal Association
Example	Nonexample

Figure 3.8: Blank vocabulary organizer template.

Teach Cognates

Learning *cognates*, English words that are closely related in meaning and origin to words in the student's primary language, is especially helpful to Spanish-speaking students and others for whom the primary language is rooted in Latin, and to a lesser extent, Greek. For example, consider these cognates:

formas forms *papel* paper *igual* equal *cubo* cube

(See appendix B, page 137, for a list of some common English-Spanish math cognates.) Word matches and puzzles are useful tools in helping students recognize similarities in language (see fig. 3.9).

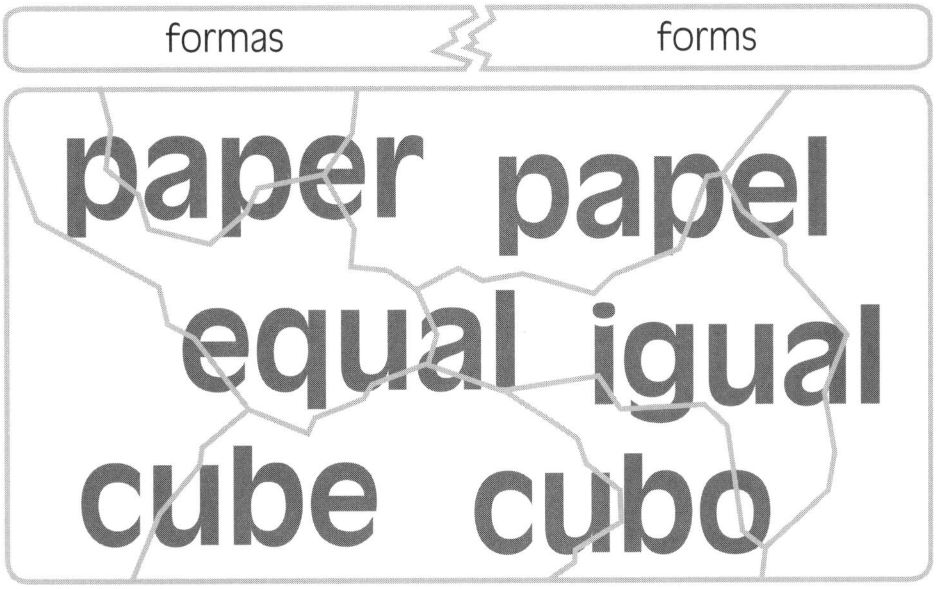

formas ⚡ forms

paper papel

equal igual

cube cubo

Figure 3.9: Sample word matches and puzzles.

Use Word Sorts

If students can categorize words, they are likely to comprehend. *Word sorts* are activities that help students learn to organize concepts mentally. Provide a word bank, and prompt students to sort the words into categories (see table 3.3, page 56). Allow students to define their own categories; use questioning strategies only as necessary when they are having difficulty.

Sample Sort

Word bank:

ounce, cup, millimeter, pound, foot, pint, mile, gallon, inch, gram, meter, liter, ton, yard, milliliter, kilogram, kilometer, fluid ounce

Table 3.3: Sample Word Sort

Length	Mass and Weight	Capacity
Millimeter	Gram	Milliliter
Meter	Kilogram	Liter
Kilometer	Ounce	Fluid ounce
Inch	Pound	Cup
Foot	Ton	Pint
Yard		Quart
Mile		Gallon

Use Find Someone Who

In Find Someone Who, students find someone who can explain one of the given words. They ask him or her to write the definition, draw the representation, and then sign his or her name (see table 3.4). Students may not use the same person for more than one word.

Table 3.4: Find Someone Who Chart

Word	Definition	Picture	Signature
Acute angle			
Obtuse angle			
Right angle			
Parallel lines			
Intersecting lines			
Perpendicular lines			

Task: Choosing Appropriate Linguistic Strategies

Refer back to the case studies of Anh, Luca, Pakiza, Camilo, and Lin. Determine which linguistic practices and possible activities you would use to encourage understanding, participating, and communicating. Write your responses in the space provided. After completing your work, compare your answers to those on page 149.

> ### Reflection 3.2
> How might you use the vocabulary development practices and activities discussed in this chapter in your classroom? Compare your answers to those on page 149.

Case Study: Anh

Anh and her parents are immigrants from Vietnam. Anh has many friends and attempts to converse with them in English but must watch closely for facial expressions and gestures to give her clues about what they are saying. Her computational skills in mathematics are excellent, but she is easily frustrated when trying to solve contextual problems.

How many different perimeters can a rectangle have if its area is equal to 24 square inches? Explain your thinking.

Area

Perimeter	Side	Side	Area
10	4	6	24
14	12	2	24
25	24	1	24
11	3	8	24

Answer: 8

Beginning   Early Intermediate   Intermediate   Advanced   Proficient

Case Study: Luca

Luca moved to Canada three years ago from Italy, where he attended a private school. He has an older brother in high school. Idioms and slang sometimes confuse Luca, but he communicates easily in descriptive English, readily learns concepts in his mathematics class, and communicates using appropriate academic language.

> How many different perimeters can a rectangle have if its area is equal to 24 square inches? Explain your thinking.
>
> If area = length x width, then 24 could be 1 x 24, 2 x 12, 4 x 6, or 3 x 8. If you make those numbers the sides, you get 1 + 1 + 24 + 24, 2 + 2 + 12 + 12, 4 + 4 + 6 + 6, 3 + 3 + 8 + 8. A rectangle with an area of 24 square inches can have 4 different perimeters. They are 50 inches, 28 inches, 20, and 22 inches.

Beginning　　　　Early Intermediate　　　　Intermediate　　　　Advanced　　　　Proficient

Case Study: *Pakiza*

Pakiza and her family recently emigrated from Pakistan. She is frequently absent from school and, when in class, relies on pictures, gestures, and translations by her bilingual friends for both understanding and communication.

How many different perimeters can a rectangle have if its area is equal to 24 square inches? Explain your thinking.

$$
\begin{array}{r}
24 \\
\times\ 24 \\
\hline
96 \\
+\ 480 \\
\hline
576\ \text{inches}
\end{array}
$$

Beginning   Early Intermediate   Intermediate   Advanced   Proficient

Case Study: Camilo

Camilo and his mother came to the United States from Guatemala two years ago. He can read unmodified texts with occasional assistance. He converses easily in English, using some descriptive language. He can communicate ideas in mathematics class, especially when working with a cooperative group. Although he passed his mathematics and reading cumulative assessments, he did not pass the writing assessment.

How many different perimeters can a rectangle have if its area is equal to 24 square inches? Explain your thinking.

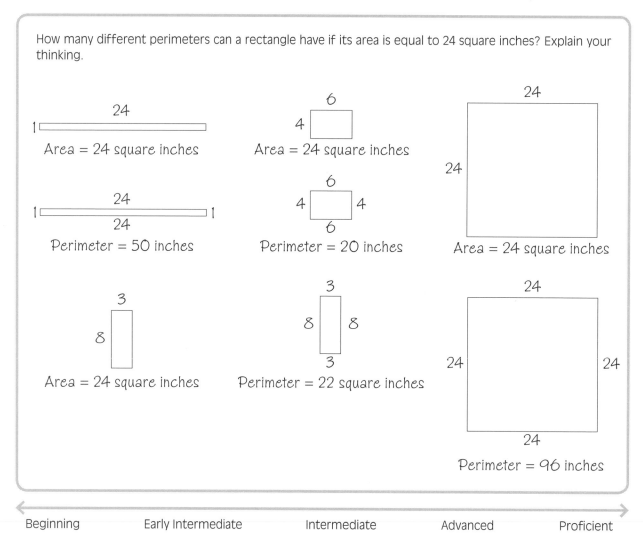

Beginning   Early Intermediate   Intermediate   Advanced   Proficient

Case Study: Lin

Fourteen months ago, Lin and his family left China and settled in Vancouver, where several of his relatives live. They provide encouragement and support to Lin and his parents. He relies on modified texts in reading and social studies and does well in math despite the unavailability of a modified text. He has difficulty with contextual problems but seeks help from his teacher and fellow students.

How many different perimeters can a rectangle have if its area is equal to 24 square inches? Explain your thinking.

$1 \times 24 = 24$ area

Width = 1

Length = 24

$1 + 1 + 24 + 24 = 50$ perimeter

$2 \times 12 = 24$ area

Width = 2

Length = 12

$2 + 2 + 12 + 12 = 28$ perimeter

$3 \times 8 = 24$ area

Length = 8

Width = 3

$3 + 3 + 8 + 8 = 22$ perimeter

$4 \times 6 = 24$ area

Length = 6

Width = 4

$4 + 4 + 6 + 6 = 20$ perimeter

Beginning   Early Intermediate   Intermediate   Advanced   Proficient

BIG IDEAS

- Mathematics text is denser than other texts and requires unique knowledge and skills not taught in other areas.

- The syntax of word problems—pronouns, prepositions, reversals, conditional sentences, and passive voice—makes them more difficult for English language learners to understand.

- Abstractions, multiple meanings, and embedded concepts also make understanding the language of mathematics difficult.

- The student's background, prior knowledge, and primary language development influence the rate at which he or she will become proficient in English and mathematics.

- Cognates can be useful in helping Spanish-speaking students (or speakers of any of the Romance languages) understand that they know more English than they thought because there are so many similarities between English and the Romance languages.

Points to Ponder

Do you know whether your English language learners understand both social language and the language of mathematics?

Are your English language learners actively engaged in learning mathematics, regardless of their language proficiency?

Are you providing a variety of modalities to encourage communication at the highest level each ELL is capable of producing?

Providing Cognitive Supports for English Language Learners

The true spirit of delight, the exaltation, the sense of being more than Man, which is the touchstone of the highest excellence, is to be found in mathematics as surely as in poetry.

—Bertrand Russell

In chapter 2, we looked at factors that affect language acquisition. Since the factor over which educators have the most control is the quality of instruction, we will continue to emphasize the importance of the role of the mathematics teacher as we look at increasing student understanding, participating, and communicating. In much the same way that we examined how to provide linguistic supports for language acquisition in chapter 3, here we will examine how to provide cognitive supports for the development of the skills, conceptual understanding, and thought processes that lead to mathematical proficiency.

When students encounter a word problem, they must not only read the text but also decode the mathematics involved. They must determine relevant concepts, including whether there is extraneous information, and decide which operations to use on any numbers.

Task: Determining Mathematical Obstacles

Let's return to the problem presented in chapter 3. Study figures 4.1–4.5 on the following pages to identify the mathematical concepts the student might be able to determine about the problem. Do you think the student could solve the problem? Justify your response in the space provided. After completing your work, compare your answers to those on page 150.

_____ ____ _ the ____ _____ store _ _____ _ new ____ __ __ ____ ____. The
_____ store ___ 2 ____ ___ 3 _____ _____ __ ___.

_____ __ _ _ the _____ _____ ___ _ ____ ___ ____ ___ _____?

Figure 4.1: Comprehension at beginning proficiency.

Could a beginning-level student solve this problem? Why or why not? What mathematical concepts could he or she determine at this level of proficiency?

Candace _____ _ the ____ _____ store _ _____ a new ____ __ her piano _____. The
_____ store ___ 2 skirts and 3 sweaters _____ _ her ___.

What ___ all __ the different _____ __ _____ ___ Candace ___ _____?

Figure 4.2: Comprehension at early intermediate proficiency.

Could an early intermediate-level student solve this problem? Why or why not? What mathematical concepts could he or she determine at this level of proficiency?

Candace went to the local department store to purchase a new outfit ___ her piano _____. The department store had 2 skirts and 3 sweaters _____ in her size.

What are all of the different _____ of outfits that Candace can purchase?

Figure 4.3: Comprehension at intermediate proficiency.

Could an intermediate-level student solve this problem? Why or why not? What mathematical concepts could he or she determine at this level of proficiency?

Candace went to the local department store to purchase a new outfit ___ her piano _____. The department store had 2 skirts and 3 sweaters _____ in her size.

What are all of the different _____ of outfits that Candace can purchase?

Figure 4.4: Comprehension at advanced proficiency.

Could an advanced-level student solve this problem? Why or why not? What mathematical concepts could he or she determine at this level of proficiency?

Candace went to the local department store to purchase a new outfit for her piano recital. The department store had 2 skirts and 3 sweaters available in her size.

What are all of the different combinations of outfits that Candace can purchase?

Figure 4.5: Comprehension at English proficiency.

Could a proficient student solve this problem? Why or why not? What mathematical concepts could he or she determine at this level of proficiency?

Mathematics Obstacles

In addition to the obstacles English language learners face in learning the language of mathematics, many immigrant students come from schools where concepts and skills may have been taught or emphasized differently than in their new school (Haynes, 2003). Some examples of those differences are:

- Commas and decimal points may be interchanged. For example, 67.225,53 is the same as 67,225.53.

- Numerals may be formed differently. It is not infrequent for students to cross the numeral *7*, written as 7̶, or to write the numeral *9* as ꝯ. It is more problematic when the numerals are vastly different. For instance, *3* is written ٣ and pronounced *thalatha* in Arabic.

- Arithmetic operations may be performed using different algorithms (see figure 4.6). If the number in the one's place of the bottom number is greater than the number above it, subtract the bottom number from 10, and add the result. Then adjust by adding 1 to the number in the ten's place of the bottom number. Then subtract. (The academic vocabulary word for the top number is *minuend* and for the bottom number is *subtrahend*.)

- Divisors and dividends may be expressed differently. For example, in some countries, *a divided by b* is written *a : b*, whereas in the United States and in Canada, the colon is restricted to expressing ratios. Many students are unfamiliar with the obelus (÷).

Step 1	Step 4
9 4 -3 8 The digit 8 is greater than the digit above it (4).	9 4 -3 8 ——— 6 Write the result (6) in the one's place of the answer.
Step 2 10 − 8 = 2 Subtract 8 from 10.	Step 5 9 4 ⁴3 8 ——— 6 To compensate for using 10 when we subtracted, add 1 to the ten's digit (3) and subtract.
Step 3 2 + 4 = 6 Add the result (2) to the top digit in the one's place (4).	

Figure 4.6: Example of an alternate subtraction style.

- The metric system may be used exclusively, which greatly decreases the need for learning fractions.
- Manipulatives may not have been used.
- Estimation may not have been emphasized.
- Concept development may have been stressed far more than computational skills, or vice versa.
- Geometry is not emphasized in some countries.

It is helpful to be aware that there are differences in prior knowledge, but it is sometimes difficult to determine whether students are struggling with the language or with the concept. We already know that ELLs are hesitant to volunteer to respond in front of the whole class and risk the embarrassment of not-yet-proficient language, even if they understand the mathematics. So how do we know if they are "getting it"?

> One person's constant is another person's variable.
> —Susan Gerhart

Reflection 4.1

In the margin, describe some of the actions you have observed from English language learners who don't understand a mathematical concept. In what ways do they compensate for not understanding? Compare your answers to those on page 150.

Overcoming Mathematics Obstacles

We know students learn more efficiently when we connect content to prior knowledge. Therefore, planning how to tap into that prior knowledge as an introduction to the lesson is an important step in ensuring students will be successful in learning any new concepts. But what if they do not have the necessary background knowledge to succeed in the lesson? Then, put very simply, we must build background so all students have a common starting point. Manipulatives and *realia* (real-life objects) are especially helpful in building background and accelerating understanding.

There are many ways to check for student understanding, including nonverbal clues such as body language and facial expressions that indicate "I got it!" or "I haven't got a clue about this." Asking the student to explain his or her strategies and reasoning in the primary language to a bilingual student who can then translate and help draw the beginning-level student into the discussion can help you determine whether the student understands the language and concepts. Since a bilingual student is not always available, you will want to use nonverbal forms of communication. Beginning students can also show they understand by choosing from examples and nonexamples. Asking the student to make a sketch, graph, table, chart, or other representation lets him or her demonstrate understanding nonverbally.

To accelerate the learning process, do the following:

- Teach each student to be aware of his or her own thinking.

- Help each student discover that problems can be solved in a variety of ways.

- Encourage each student to find errors and to discuss why the errors occurred (Secada & de la Cruz, 1996).

When you introduce new concepts or when you determine the student does not understand a concept, draw from tools and strategies that encourage mathematical learning. Table 4.1 summarizes these tools and strategies.

Table 4.1: Cognitive Strategies to Increase Understanding, Participating, and Communicating

Proficiency Level	Understanding	Participating	Communicating

Beginning	• Connect learning to prior knowledge.
	• Provide ample wait time.
	• Employ an ESL teacher, a bilingual teacher or aides, and/or parent volunteers to provide short prelessons, not direct translations of the lesson.
	• Use and teach students to use tools such as calculators with graphing capabilities.
		• Encourage students to work together.
		• Use manipulatives and visuals to model methods for problem solving.
		• Use and teach students to use tools such as calculators with graphing capabilities.
		• Limit length of assignments.
		• Provide primary language support if possible.
			• Provide opportunities for students to engage in mathematical discourse even if nonverbal:
			  ‣ Teacher to student
			  ‣ Student to teacher
			  ‣ Student to student
			• Allow students to demonstrate knowledge using tables, graphs, charts, and pictures.
			• Extend response time.
			• Ask for thumbs up/thumbs down responses.
			• Create assessments as free from bias as possible.

Early Intermediate	*Continue to use the strategies listed above, and:* • Connect learning to prior knowledge. • Use comparing and contrasting to accelerate understanding. • Provide meaningful contexts related to the student's background. • Provide simplified notes with pictures. • Modify texts and activities to reflect similar language, but do *not* simplify the content. • Include tables, graphs, charts, and drawings to assist students in understanding posed problems.	*Continue to use the strategies listed above as needed, and:* • Use games that reinforce concepts. • Assign projects for students to work with a partner or small group.	*Continue to use the strategies listed above as needed, and:* • Use dry erase boards, which can be easily cut from bathroom tileboard. • Create assessments that measure mathematical understanding, not reading proficiency. • Assess using alternative methods such as group projects, rubrics, checklists, journals, and portfolios.
Intermediate	*Continue to use the strategies listed above as needed, and:* • Ask scaffolding questions. • Use multiple representations in problem solving. • Provide partially completed examples.	*Continue to use the strategies listed above as needed, and:* • Provide opportunities for students to think about their thinking: *How do you know that? Why did you decide it was not . . . ?* • Teach test-taking and study skills.	*Continue to use the strategies listed above as needed, and:* • Emphasize thoughtful, quality responses. • Ask students to justify answers using tables, graphs, drawings, and a few words or short phrases in English.

continued on next page →

Proficiency Level	Understanding	Participating	Communicating
Advanced	*Continue to use the strategies listed above as needed, and:* • Encourage students to develop their own study guides.	*Continue to use the strategies listed above as needed.*	*Continue to use the strategies listed above as needed, and:* • Ask questions that require more lengthy explanations. • Ask questions that require more complex knowledge of the language of mathematics. • Ask students to verify answers in English using complete sentences to explain tables, graphs, drawings, and so on.
Proficient	*Continue to use the strategies listed above as needed.*	*Continue to use the strategies listed above as needed.*	*Continue to use the strategies listed above as needed, and:* • Prompt students to justify answers using complex sentences with correct grammar, descriptive language, and academic vocabulary.

Tools and Activities for Understanding, Participating, and Communicating

Figures 4.7, 4.8, 4.9, and 4.10 (page 72) show some examples of mathematics tools and strategies. Manipulatives such as counters to model operations, blocks for building volume models and viewing three-dimensional objects, patty paper for geometry transformations and definitions, isometric dot paper, plastic polygons, geoboards, and realia (real-life objects) provide essential connections for all learners.

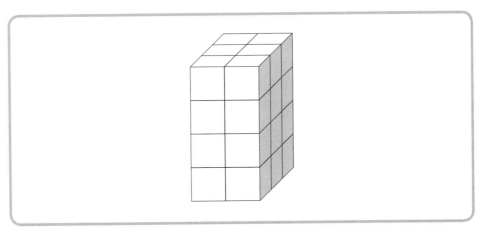

Figure 4.7: This concrete model approximates cubic units in order to determine the volume of a given container or other three-dimensional geometric figure.

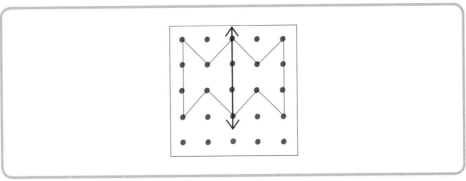

Figure 4.8: A geoboard can be used to create two-dimensional figures with lines of symmetry.

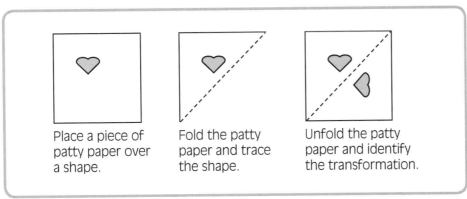

Place a piece of patty paper over a shape.

Fold the patty paper and trace the shape.

Unfold the patty paper and identify the transformation.

Figure 4.9: Patty paper can be used to demonstrate transformations.

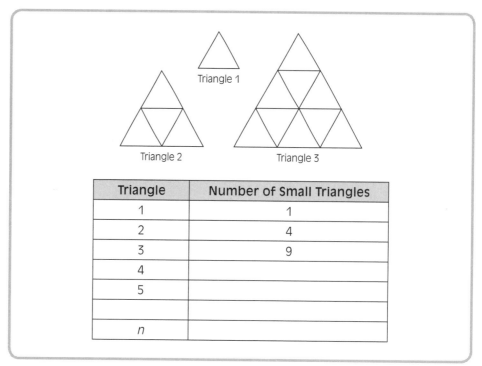

Triangle	Number of Small Triangles
1	1
2	4
3	9
4	
5	
n	

Figure 4.10: Pattern blocks can be used to explore patterns.

Concepts can be reinforced or reviewed using *example/nonexample t-charts*. These charts also can serve as an informal assessment; the student completes the table by writing in examples and nonexamples that support the concept defined in the heading (see table 4.2). To introduce example/nonexample t-charts, post a chart with the examples filled in, and, as a whole-class activity, ask students to respond with nonexamples.

Table 4.2: Sample T-Chart

Prime Numbers	
Example	*Nonexample*
3	9
5	15
11	24

Write or print sets of examples and nonexamples of several concepts on card stock. Cut apart and place each set in a different baggie. Give each group a different bagged set, and ask students to sort them into examples and nonexamples and to determine the concept they describe. Then ask groups to reproduce their results on chart paper, butcher paper, a transparency, or even on the back of a book cover. Then have them display their work and share their findings.

The child's game Who Am I? uses comparing and contrasting to develop understanding of a particular concept. A word bank is an appropriate adaptation for beginning, early intermediate, and intermediate English language learners. To be most effective with ELLs, draw a t-chart or table with columns for *Yes* and *No*. Then list hints such as those following which students will say, write, and, when possible, use gestures to demonstrate. See table 4.3 for an example.

Table 4.3: Sample Who Am I? Game Hints

Yes	No
My capacity is equal to 4 quarts.	I am not used to measure temperature.
I am used to measure capacity.	I am not smaller than a cup.
My capacity is greater than a pint.	I am not used to measure time.

HOT TIP!

Make a template for Who Am I? and example/nonexample t-charts on overhead transparencies or computer-projected slides to use as a short end-of-class closing.

The answer to table 4.3 is a *gallon*. After responding to Who Am I? and example/nonexample activities several times, students "catch on" and enjoy playing the role of the teacher.

Window panes can be used to explore related concepts. In this case, the students are given a problem and asked to fill in each of the panes (see figure 4.11). As with any organizer, phase in window panes with think-alouds and modeling, followed by group work, before asking individual students to complete the activity independently.

Tyrone equally separated his 36 toy cars onto 4 shelves. How many toy cars did he place on each shelf?

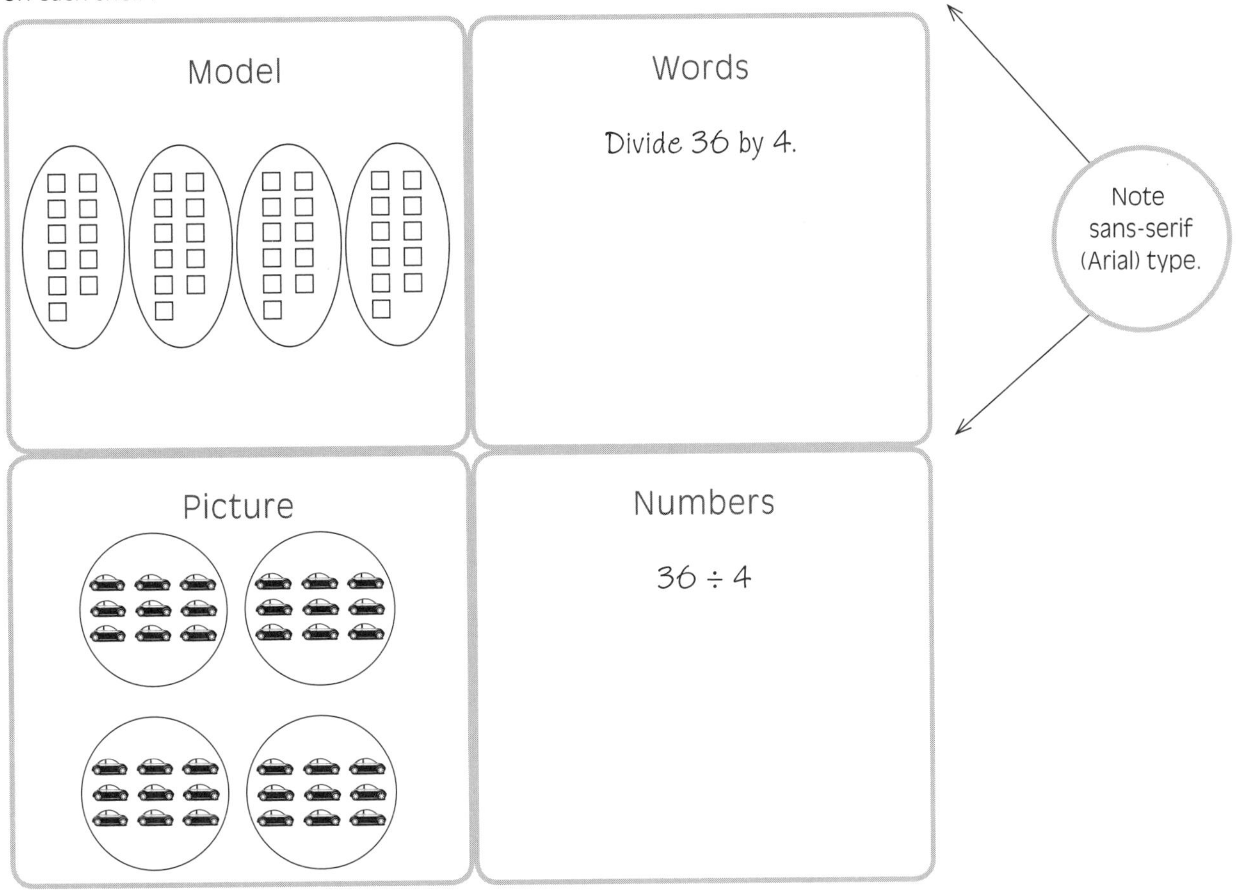

Figure 4.11: Sample window panes organizer.

It is important for students to represent and make connections among multiple representations of problem situations. In a graphic organizer such as the *four-quadrant problem solver* in figure 4.12, the student is given one of the four representations and fills in the other three. You can further enhance learning by asking students to represent the four quadrants on chart paper. After posting their work, groups can share their work during a "gallery tour."

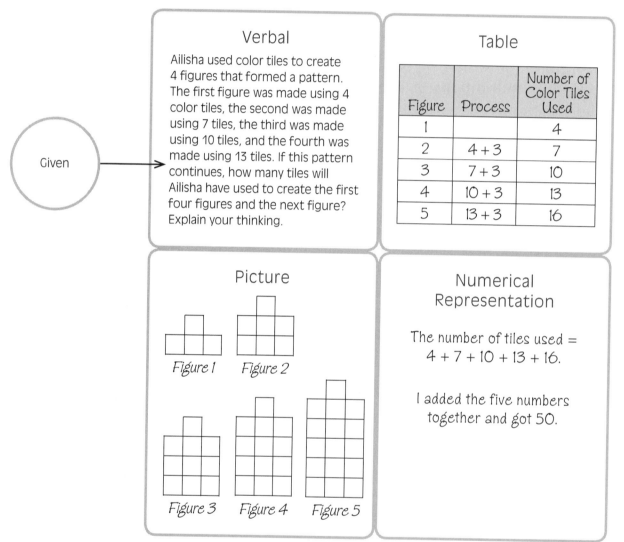

Figure 4.12: Sample four-quadrant problem solver.

Another example of a problem-solving organizer is the *See-Plan-Do-Reflect* model shown in figure 4.13 (adapted from Polya, 1957).

It is also important to incorporate instructional practices that encourage the student's metacognitive development. Metacognitive practices help students become more aware of their own mental processes during problem solving. That awareness, in turn, contributes to the classroom becoming an environment of cooperation and inquiry, enhancing all students' abilities to work both independently and interdependently. The following metacognitive activity provides an opportunity for students to compare and contrast their ideas and thought processes with others.

Figure 4.13: Sample See-Plan-Do-Reflect.

Bonded Brains helps students structure their work within and between groups in order to converse and learn. For example, arrange the class in groups of four or five. Each group works a given problem that has one correct answer but multiple ways of getting to it. Assign numbers to the students so that no two members of the same group have the same number; the students will form new groups of four or five. After the groups have completed the problem, prompt the one to form a new group. The two form a second new group, and so on. After the new groups discuss the problem and complete the Bonded Brains activity sheet (see table 4.4), they return to their home groups, debrief each other, and make any revisions they would like to their original work.

Table 4.4: A Bonded Brains Worksheet

My Group's Ideas	Ideas From Other Groups
	Which ideas did all the groups have in common?
	Which ideas were different?
	What did I learn from members of other groups?

Task: Choosing Appropriate Tools and Activities

Now we will again visit the case studies. Consider the work sample and description of each student on the following pages.

Which of this chapter's tools and activities would you use with each of the students in the case studies? Would you use the tool or activity to encourage understanding, participating, or communicating? You may want to refer to table 4.1, Cognitive Strategies to Increase Understanding, Participating, and Communicating (pages 69–70) to guide your responses. Use table 4.5 to collect your responses. After completing your work, compare your answers to those on page 150.

Table 4.5: Aligning Mathematics Strategies With Specific Student Needs

Student Name	Activity	Manipulatives	Example/ Nonexample	Who Am I?	Window Panes	Four-Quadrant Problem Solver	See-Plan-Do-Reflect	Bonded Brains
Ahn	Understanding							
	Participating							
	Communicating							
Luca	Understanding							
	Participating							
	Communicating							
Pakiza	Understanding							
	Participating							
	Communicating							
Camilo	Understanding							
	Participating							
	Communicating							
Lin	Understanding							
	Participating							
	Communicating							

Reflection 4.2

Referring to table 4.5, which practices, tools, and activities would you use if you had all five case-study students in the same class? Compare your answers to those on page 151.

Case Study: Anh

Anh and her parents are immigrants from Vietnam. Anh has many friends and attempts to converse with them in English but must watch closely for facial expressions and gestures to give her clues about what they are saying. Her computational skills in mathematics are excellent, but she is easily frustrated when trying to solve contextual problems.

How many different perimeters can a rectangle have if its area is equal to 24 square inches? Explain your thinking.

Area

Perimeter	Side	Side	Area
10	4	6	24
14	12	2	24
25	24	1	24
11	3	8	24

Answer: 8

Beginning   Early Intermediate   Intermediate   Advanced   Proficient

Student Name	Activity	Manipulatives	Example/ Nonexample	Who Am I?	Window Panes	Four-Quadrant Problem Solver	See-Plan-Do-Reflect	Bonded Brains
Ahn	Understanding							
	Participating							
	Communicating							

Case Study: Luca

Luca moved to Canada three years ago from Italy, where he attended a private school. He has an older brother in high school. Idioms and slang sometimes confuse Luca, but he communicates easily in descriptive English, readily learns concepts in his mathematics class, and communicates using appropriate academic language.

How many different perimeters can a rectangle have if its area is equal to 24 square inches? Explain your thinking.

If area = length x width, then 24 could be 1 x 24, 2 x 12, 4 x 6, or 3 x 8. If you make those numbers the sides, you get 1 + 1 + 24 + 24, 2 + 2 + 12 + 12, 4 + 4 + 6 + 6, 3 + 3 + 8 + 8. A rectangle with an area of 24 square inches can have 4 different perimeters. They are 50 inches, 28 inches, 20, and 22 inches.

Beginning Early Intermediate Intermediate Advanced Proficient

Student Name	Activity	Manipulatives	Example/ Nonexample	Who Am I?	Window Panes	Four-Quadrant Problem Solver	See-Plan-Do-Reflect	Bonded Brains
Luca	Understanding							
	Participating							
	Communicating							

Case Study: Pakiza

Pakiza and her family recently emigrated from Pakistan. She is frequently absent from school and, when in class, relies on pictures, gestures, and translations by her bilingual friends for both understanding and communication.

How many different perimeters can a rectangle have if its area is equal to 24 square inches? Explain your thinking.

$$
\begin{array}{r}
24 \\
\times\ 24 \\
\hline
96 \\
+\ 480 \\
\hline
576\ \text{inches}
\end{array}
$$

← Beginning   Early Intermediate   Intermediate   Advanced   Proficient →

Student Name	Activity	Manipulatives	Example/ Nonexample	Who Am I?	Window Panes	Four-Quadrant Problem Solver	See-Plan-Do-Reflect	Bonded Brains
Pakiza	Understanding							
	Participating							
	Communicating							

Case Study: Camilo

Camilo and his mother came to the United States from Guatemala two years ago. He can read unmodified texts with occasional assistance. He converses easily in English, using some descriptive language. He can communicate ideas in mathematics class, especially when working with a cooperative group. Although he passed his mathematics and reading cumulative assessments, he did not pass the writing assessment.

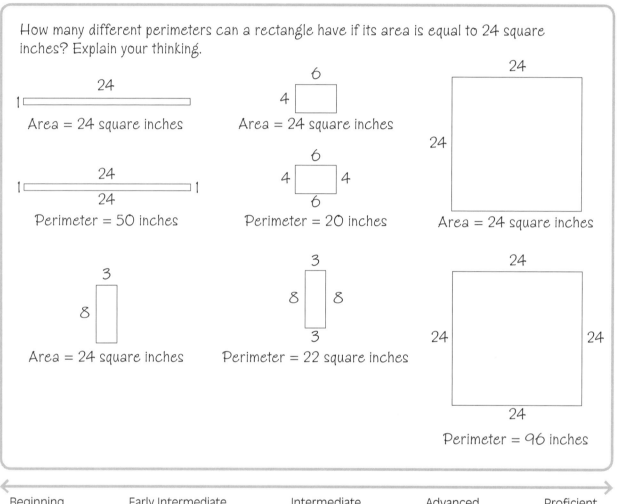

Student Name	Activity	Manipulatives	Example/ Nonexample	Who Am I?	Window Panes	Four-Quadrant Problem Solver	See-Plan-Do-Reflect	Bonded Brains
Camilo	Understanding							
	Participating							
	Communicating							

Case Study: Lin

Fourteen months ago, Lin and his family left China and settled in Vancouver, where several of his relatives live. They provide encouragement and support to Lin and his parents. He relies on modified texts in reading and social studies and does well in math despite the unavailability of a modified text. He has difficulty with contextual problems but seeks help from his teacher and fellow students.

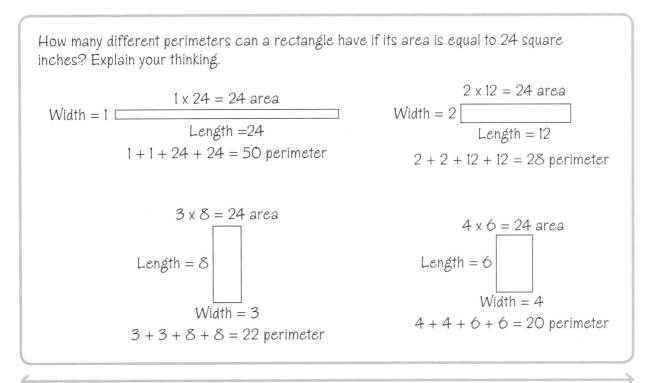

Beginning — Early Intermediate — Intermediate — Advanced — Proficient

Student Name	Activity	Manipulatives	Example/ Nonexample	Who Am I?	Window Panes	Four-Quadrant Problem Solver	See-Plan-Do-Reflect	Bonded Brains
Lin	Understanding							
	Participating							
	Communicating							

The Importance of Authentic Assessments for English Language Learners

Assessment can be informal or formal but should be linked to curriculum and instruction, used as an instrument to direct future instruction, and be as free of bias as possible. Assessment should be authentic and directly reflect student learning (McLaughlin, 1993).

According to McLaughlin, an essential part of *authentic assessment* is application to real-life situations in which students participate in meaningful tasks. Authentic assessment is frequently multidimensional in that it uses more than one piece of evidence. Students are encouraged to exhibit their thought processes through writing and representations such as charts, graphs, and tables. A rubric is generally used to ascertain student progress.

The problem used in the student case studies is an example of an authentic assessment, or performance assessment, and could be scored using a rubric such as the one in table 4.6 (page 84).

Using Rubrics to Assess Student Performance

The National Council of Teachers of Mathematics (2000) and the National Research Council (2002) believe that thinking mathematically encompasses the development of students' (1) conceptual knowledge, (2) procedural knowledge, and (3) communication skills (the ability to communicate mathematically). These are the three criteria on which to center student instruction and assess student performance in tools such as rubrics.

Conceptual Knowledge

Conceptual knowledge is the knowledge of *what*. To show conceptual knowledge, students demonstrate their understanding of the connections and relationships among different pieces of information (National Council of Teachers of Mathematics, 2000). A proficient student correctly identifies the attributes of the problem that lead him or her to correct inferences and combines the critical attributes of the problem in order to describe correctly the mathematical relationship(s) inherent in the problem. This criterion aligns with the National Research Council's (2001) first proficiency, *conceptual understanding*, of what it means for anyone to learn mathematics successfully.

Procedural Knowledge

Procedural knowledge is the knowledge of *how*. To show procedural knowledge, students demonstrate their understanding of skills, algorithms (computational procedures), techniques, and methods in determining and using strategies to solve the problem (National Council of Teachers of Mathematics, 2000). A proficient student correctly selects and implements an appropriate strategy, uses an appropriate representation to connect the procedure to the concept of the problem, and correctly implements the procedure to arrive at a correct solution to the problem. This criterion aligns with the National Research Council's (2001) second and third proficiencies, *procedural fluency* and *strategic competence*, of what it means for anyone to learn mathematics successfully.

Communication Skills

The ability to communicate mathematically shows knowledge of *why*. To demonstrate the ability to communicate mathematically, students provide clear, detailed, and organized analyses to justify the solution, using correct terminology and notation (National Council of Teachers of Mathematics, 2000). The presentation of the solution clearly demonstrates the thinking process. A proficient student fully answers the question of *why* for the selected strategy, explains the procedure he or she used, and evaluates the solution for reasonableness using age-appropriate terminology and notation. This criterion aligns with the National Research Council's (2001) fourth proficiency, *adaptive reasoning*, of what it means for anyone to learn mathematics successfully.

The rubrics in tables 4.6 (page 84) and 4.7 (page 85) measure these three criteria: what it means to be able to understand, know, and do mathematics. Notice the first rubric is for teacher use, and the second rubric is for student use to assess their own work. Rubric results can be reported using a chart like the one in table 4.8 (page 85). Circle *Yes* or *No* on the first line depending on whether the answer is correct. Then using the rubric, determine whether the conceptual knowledge, procedural knowledge, and communication skills align to the descriptor for 1, 2, 3, or 4 "points," and place a check or *X* in the appropriate box of the scoring document.

Table 4.6: Mathematics Performance Assessment Rubric (Teacher Form)

Correct Solution? Yes   No

Criteria	4	3	2	1
Conceptual knowledge	**Attribute(s)** Correctly identifies attributes of the problem, which justifies correct inferences	**Attribute(s)** Correctly identifies most attributes of the problem, which leads to correct inferences	**Attribute(s)** Identifies some of the attributes of the problem, which leads to partially correct inferences	**Attribute(s)** Lacks identification of any of the critical attributes of the problem
	Inferences Combines the critical attributes of the problem in order to correctly describe the mathematical relationship(s) inherent in the problem	**Inferences** Combines the critical attributes of the problem, which leads to a partial identification of the mathematical relationship(s) inherent in the problem	**Inferences** Combines the identified attributes of the problem, which leads to a partial identification of the mathematical relationship(s) inherent in the problem	**Inferences** Combines few of the attributes of the problem, which leads to an incomplete identification of the mathematical relationship(s) inherent in the problem
Procedural knowledge	**Strategy** Selects and implements an appropriate strategy	**Strategy** Selects and implements an appropriate strategy, with only one or two minor flaws	**Strategy** Selects and implements a partially appropriate strategy	**Strategy** Selects and implements an inappropriate strategy
	Representational Form Uses appropriate representation to connect the procedure to the concept of the problem	**Representational Form** Uses appropriate representation to connect the procedure to the concept of the problem, with only one or two minor flaws	**Representational Form** Uses inconsistent or insufficient representation for the selected solution strategy	**Representational Form** Uses incorrect representation
	Algorithmic Competency Correctly implements a procedure to arrive at a correct solution	**Algorithmic Competency** Implements the selected procedure but arrives at an incorrect solution because of a careless error	**Algorithmic Competency** Implements the selected procedure but arrives at an incorrect solution	**Algorithmic Competency** Makes significant errors
Communication skills	**Justification** Fully answers the question of *why* for the strategy selection, explains the procedure, and/or evaluates the reasonableness of the solution	**Justification** Incompletely answers the question of *why* for the strategy selection, or incompletely explains the procedure and/or evaluates the reasonableness of the solution	**Justification** Incompletely answers the question of *why* for the strategy selection, and only partially explains the procedure and/or evaluates the reasonableness of the solution	**Justification** Provides very little or no explanation of what was done and why
	Terminology Uses appropriate terminology and notation	**Terminology** Uses mostly appropriate terminology and notation	**Terminology** Uses some appropriate terminology or notation	**Terminology** Uses limited or inappropriate terminology or notation

Table 4.7: Mathematics Performance Assessment Rubric (Student Form)

Criteria	4	3	2	1
Concept • Understand the problem.	• I understood how all of the parts of the problem fit together, so I could make sense of the problem.	• I understood all of the parts of the problem, and I made partial sense of the problem.	• I understood some of the parts of the problem.	• I showed little to no understanding of the important facts of the problem that would help me find the answer.
Procedure • Work the problem.	• I used an appropriate strategy. • I connected how I needed to do the problem with what I understood about the problem and my selected strategy. • I did all of my math steps correctly.	• I used an appropriate strategy. • I connected how I needed to do the problem with what I understood about the problem and my selected strategy. • I did some of my math steps correctly. I did not arrive at a correct solution.	• I used an appropriate strategy. • I showed little connection between how I needed to do the problem and my selected strategy. • I did some of my math steps correctly but reached an incorrect or correct solution.	• I used an inappropriate strategy. • My work had lots of mistakes.
Communication • Communicate what you understand. • Communicate how you worked the problem.	• I explained why I did what I did and supported my explanation with information from the problem. • I used correct math vocabulary and notation.	• I explained why I did what I did and supported my explanation with information from the problem. • I used some correct math vocabulary and notation.	• I gave little explanation of why I did what I did. • I only explained what I did. • I used some correct math vocabulary and notation.	• I gave very little or no explanation of what I did. • I used little or incorrect math vocabulary and/or notation.

I arrived at a correct solution.   Yes   No

Table 4.8: Reporting Rubric Results

Student arrived at a correct solution: Yes No	4	3	2	1
Conceptual knowledge				
Procedural knowledge				
Communication skills				

Task: Using Rubrics for Evaluation

Now we will use the rubric from table 4.6 to evaluate the work in each of five student case studies. After completing your work, compare your answers to those on page 151.

Anh

Student arrived at a correct solution: Yes No				
	4	3	2	1
Conceptual knowledge				
Procedural knowledge				
Communication skills				

Luca

Student arrived at a correct solution: Yes No				
	4	3	2	1
Conceptual knowledge				
Procedural knowledge				
Communication skills				

Pakiza

Student arrived at a correct solution: Yes No				
	4	3	2	1
Conceptual knowledge				
Procedural knowledge				
Communication skills				

Camilo

Student arrived at a correct solution: Yes No				
	4	3	2	1
Conceptual knowledge				
Procedural knowledge				
Communication skills				

Lin

Student arrived at a correct solution: Yes No				
	4	3	2	1
Conceptual knowledge				
Procedural knowledge				
Communication skills				

The data gathered from a rubric used to score a performance assessment early in the year can serve as a baseline to evaluate learning as the year progresses. It is important to remember students should be allowed to communicate in ways appropriate to their proficiency levels. Performance assessments should be gradually implemented, first with teacher think-alouds, then with groups producing together, and only then should students complete performance assessments individually.

Suggestions for Implementing Performance Assessments

Performance assessments can be an invaluable tool to teachers in assessing student learning. Multiple-choice, fill-in-the-blank, matching, true/false, and short answer assessments are easy to grade and certainly give the teacher an idea of what the student has and has not learned. However, how much a student has learned (or not) is often not evident in these closed assessments in which the temptation to guess is great. In contrast, performance assessments have one correct answer but provide multiple ways for the student to arrive at that answer, such as by using a chart or table or by drawing a picture—opportunities to demonstrate learning that are not inherent in most standard assessments.

However, performance assessments should be implemented over time with forethought and intent. Table 4.9 outlines a process for implementing performance assessments.

Table 4.9: Implementing Performance Assessments

Round One
1. Choose an assignment that aligns with course content.
2. Complete the assessment as a class with the teacher as facilitator.
3. Provide vocabulary to the class.
4. Introduce a student rubric.
5. Score some sample classwork with the class, asking prompting questions, such as, "What would we add to this answer to make it a 3 or 4?"
6. Pass out other sample classwork.
7. Have students score samples.

Round Two
1. Have students complete the assessment in small groups.
2. Provide vocabulary to the class.
3. Have groups present their solutions to the class.
4. Have the class score the assessments together.
5. Do not record grades.

Round Three
1. Have students brainstorm the relevant vocabulary with decreasing input from the teacher.
2. Have students complete the assessment in small groups.
3. Have students self-score.
4. Score the assessments yourself.

continued on next page→

Round Three
5. Ask students to compare their self-scores with the teacher's scores and to justify their scores.
6. Do not record grades.
7. Repeat the procedures in Round Three several times before proceeding to Round Four.
Round Four
1. Have students complete the assessment individually.
2. You may still facilitate vocabulary.
3. Score the assessment.
4. Record the grades.

After students have become comfortable with performance assessments and you are ready to begin recording grades on them, it may be helpful to develop a chart similar to the one in table 4.10 to establish a consistent standard for converting the rubric scoring document to a grade on a 100-point scale.

Table 4.10: Assigning Grades to Performance Assessments

Grade	Correct Answer?	Conceptual Understanding	Procedural Understanding	Communication
100	Yes	4	4	4
95	Yes	4	4	3
95	Yes	3	4	4
95	No	4	3	4
90	Yes	3	4	3
90	No	4	3	3
90	No	3	3	4
85	No	3	3	3
80	No	3	3	2
80	No	3	2	3
80	No	2	3	3
75	No	2	2	2
70	No	2	2	1
70	No	2	1	2
70	No	1	2	2
65	No	1	1	1

Once students are familiar with how they receive grades on performance assessments, they are ready for the teacher to begin adding them to regular classroom tests. It is important to remember that students will take longer to complete a performance assessment than other tests. Include only one performance assessment per test, or use a performance assessment that encompasses all the taught concepts to determine what students have learned.

A final note about grading: timely feedback has been shown to improve learning when it gives the student specific guidance on what is right and what is wrong along with the opportunity to improve the response. If students receive only marks or grades, they do not benefit from the feedback (Marzano, 2001).

BIG IDEAS

- English language learners come from backgrounds in which the curriculum may emphasize different skills and concepts than those emphasized in U.S. and Canadian schools.

- English language learners may represent numbers and numerical relationships differently.

- Using both verbal and nonverbal clues helps determine whether students' misconceptions are language-based or concept-based.

- Using a variety of tools, strategies, and activities helps encourage students' understanding of, participation in, and communication of mathematical concepts.

- Using authentic assessments will yield a valuable view of student learning and progress.

Points to Ponder

How can you tie together supporting English language learners' affective, linguistic, and cognitive needs?

What does affective, linguistic, and cognitive support look like in a mathematics lesson?

5

Applying Strategies for ELLs: A 5E Lesson

> Learning without thought is labor lost; thought without learning is perilous.
> —Confucius

In the first four chapters, we examined the needs of English language learners and how to support them in the affective, linguistic, and cognitive domains. The question now arises of how to incorporate the tools, practices, and strategies into practical classroom use. Perhaps you are asking yourself:

- *What does a lesson look like that meets the needs of my English language learners?*

- *How can I meet the needs of my English language learners and still meet the needs of other students in my classroom?*

Echevarria, Vogt, and Short (2004) identify the critical instructional features necessary for the academic and language development of English language learners.

Lesson preparation: Planning should result in lessons that enable students to make connections between their knowledge and experiences and the new information being taught.

Background building: A student's background impacts his or her ability to recall and elaborate on a topic better than those with limited knowledge of the topic. When students lack background on a topic, the teacher intervenes to build vocabulary, connect the topic to the background the students already have, and assist students in building their own backgrounds through engaging activities and graphic organizers.

Comprehensible input: Comprehensible input involves speaking slowly, using gestures, drawing and showing pictures, providing hands-on activities, and actively building vocabulary and concept development so that students understand what is being asked of them.

Strategies: Some strategies include teaching students to be aware of their own thinking, helping them to organize the information they are expected to learn, and encouraging them to engage in group discussion or cooperative learning to solve problems and accelerate the learning process.

Student interaction: In many classrooms, there is excessive teacher talk. Instead of teachers talking and students listening or taking notes, students should be interacting as they collaboratively investigate how to solve problems.

Practical application: Students more rapidly progress in mastering content objectives when routinely provided with opportunities to engage in hands-on activities and use manipulatives, just as it is much more effective to learn to ride a bicycle by doing instead of watching someone else ride it.

Lesson delivery: The most effective teachers minimize nonproductive time. They come well prepared, possess good classroom management skills, and spend little time making announcements and returning papers. They maximize engaged time in which students actively participate in the instructional process.

Assessment: Effective teachers realize it is important to evaluate student learning throughout the lesson and to determine how well they understand the concepts and vocabulary. Determining which students are ready to move on and who needs additional instruction is at the center of effective assessment and instruction and is essential to student success.

So how do you incorporate these critical instructional features into your real-life classroom? What is a research-based instructional model that can help you structure your lesson?

Components of an Effective Lesson

An effective lesson that provides the most impact on student achievement ensures that students are actively engaged in learning as well as reflecting on their learning to make sense of the activities. Learning something new or understanding something familiar in greater depth involves making sense of both our prior experiences and firsthand knowledge gained from new explorations. An effective lesson provides opportunities to use, extend, and apply what is learned. The 5E instructional model developed and modified by Roger W. Bybee, past executive director of the National Research Council and the Center for Science, Mathematics, and Engineering Education, provides such a model. The components of the 5E instructional model (Trowbridge & Bybee, 1996) are the following:

1. **Engage**—The teacher initiates this stage by asking well-chosen questions, defining a problem to be solved, or showing something intriguing. The activity should be designed to interest students in the problem, to make connections to past and present learning, and to build common background.

2. Explore—The exploration stage directly involves students with the key concepts of the lesson through guided exploration that requires them to probe, inquire, and question. As we learn, the puzzle pieces—the ideas and concepts necessary to solve the problem—begin to fit together or need to be broken down and reconstructed several times. In this stage, the teacher observes and listens to students as they interact with each other and the activity. The teacher provides probing questions to help students clarify their understanding of major concepts and redirects the questions when necessary.

3. Explain—In the explanation stage, students should work in small groups as they begin to logically sequence events and facts from the investigation and communicate these findings to each other and the teacher. Acting as a facilitator, the teacher uses this phase to offer further explanations and provide additional meaning or information, and to formalize conceptual vocabulary. Giving labels or correct terminology is far more meaningful and helpful in retention if it is done after the learner has had a direct experience. The explanation stage is used to record the learner's development and grasp of the key ideas and concepts of the lesson.

4. Elaborate—The elaboration stage allows students to extend and expand what they have learned in the first three stages and connect this knowledge with their prior learning to create understanding. It is critical that the teacher verify student understanding during this stage.

5. Evaluate—Throughout the learning experience, the ongoing process of evaluation allows the teacher to determine whether the learner has reached the desired level of understanding of the key ideas and concepts. More formal evaluation can be conducted at this stage.

Table 5.1 summarizes how the 5E instructional model provides the components of an effective lesson.

Table 5.1: Summary of the 5E Instructional Model

Learning Phase	Lesson Preparation	Background Support	Comprehensible Input	Strategies	Student Interaction	Practical Application	Lesson Delivery	Assessment
Engage	✓	✓	✓	✓	✓		✓	
Explore	✓		✓	✓	✓	✓	✓	
Explain	✓		✓	✓	✓	✓	✓	
Elaborate	✓		✓	✓	✓	✓	✓	
Evaluate	✓			✓	✓	✓		✓

If assessments of the student's progress indicate he or she has not mastered the learning, the teacher should re-enter the student at the appropriate point in the instructional model. Reiterate connections between past and present learning covered in the Engage phase. Use different materials to reinforce concepts, processes, and skills investigated during the Explore phase. Provide additional examples to allow extended time during the Explain phase to facilitate the student's understanding of the key ideas and concepts. Guided-practice activities may need further teacher support to connect, extend, and transfer learning to new situations; you may also need to provide increased feedback.

Making Math Accessible to English Language Learners examines two mathematics lessons. In the remainder of this chapter, we will examine a 5E lesson called "Investigating Transformations" and show how its approach meets the needs of English language learners. In chapter 6, we will examine a traditional textbook lesson and show how to adapt it for English language learners.

Table 5.2 summarizes the objectives, materials, and preparation for our sample lesson on investigating transformations. See appendix D (page 153) for reproducibles to use with students for this lesson.

Table 5.2: Investigating Transformations Lesson Plan

Content Objectives	Language Objective	Study/Metacognitive Objective
Students will: • Identify and create lines of symmetry in two-dimensional geometric figures • Demonstrate translations, reflections, and rotations using concrete models • Use translations, reflections, and rotations to verify that two shapes are congruent. • Use reflections to verify that a shape has symmetry. • Sketch the results of translations, rotations, and reflections on a grid. • Identify the transformation that generates one figure from the other when given two congruent figures.	Students will speak and write using newly acquired content vocabulary.	Students will justify solutions, verbally or nonverbally, depending on proficiency level.

Materials	Preparation
For each student: • Transformation Path Directions, Symmetrical Transformations, Vocabulary Organizer, and Performance Assessment reproducible (pages 160, 162–163, 166, and 167) • Patty paper or tracing paper *For each pair of students:* • Reflection Path, Rotation Path, and Translation Path Activity Cards (pages 155–157) • Transformation Path Activity Card, Transformation Match-Up Cards, Symmetry Sort Cards, and Symmetry Sort Mat (pages 159, 161, 164, and 165) • Transformation Paths Shapes (page 158) in bags • Tangrams—two sets in two different colors, in bags • Rulers • Manila paper • Mirror *For the teacher:* • Transparency or slide of Transformation Path Activity Card	1. If sets of tangrams are not available, use the Tangram Masters (page 156) to make sets of tangrams on various colors of cardstock. Cut out the set of seven tangram pieces, and put each set in individual bags. 2. Make enough copies of the Transformation Paths Shapes on cardstock for all pairs of students. Cut out the set of three shapes, and put each set in individual bags. 3. Make a Transformation Path Activity Card master to project using an overhead or computer. 4. Read and select facilitation questions appropriate for students' needs.

Engage

The Engage phase of the lesson is designed to create student interest in tangrams.

1. Distribute two sets of tangrams (each set a different color), paper, and a ruler to each pair of students.

2. Prompt the students to place the ruler vertically in the middle of the piece of paper. (It does not matter if the paper is in a landscape or portrait orientation.)

3. Prompt Student One to use one set of tangrams to create a design on one side of the ruler. The design must fit on one half of the paper.

4. Prompt Student Two to use the second set of tangrams to create a mirror image of the design created by Student One on the opposite side of the ruler.

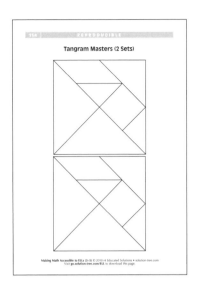

In Chinese, the tangram is called *Chi'l Ch'ae* or *wisdom board*.

Facilitation Questions: Engage Phase

Describe how you recreated your partner's design.
Answers may vary.

Are the tangram pieces on one side of the ruler in exactly the same position as the tangram pieces on the other side of the ruler? Why or why not?
No. Some pieces had to flip over or turn.

---

5. Prompt the students to remove the ruler and carefully push the two designs together to form one figure (see fig. 5.1).

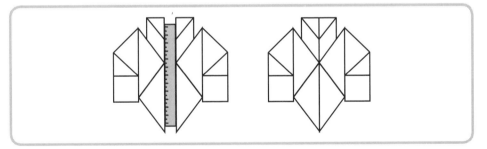

Figure 5.1: Sample tangram design.

6. Prompt the students to trace the figure carefully on the paper and cut out the entire figure in one piece.

7. Prompt the students to draw a line that represents where the two designs were joined.

8. Prompt the students to fold the figure along the line to determine whether or not the two halves of the figure are mirror images of each other.

9. Allow the students to use a mirror to check the reflection of the design created by Student One and compare it to the design created by Student Two.

10. If students' tangram designs did not create a reflection, prompt the students to repeat steps two through nine.

Table 5.3 shows how the Engage phase of this lesson supports students in understanding, participating, and communicating.

Table 5.3: Debriefing the Engage Phase of a 5E Lesson

Content Objective	Language Objective	Study/Metacognitive Objective
Understanding	*Participating*	*Communicating*
What activity will I use to stimulate curiosity and activate prior knowledge? *Students use tangrams to introduce transformations by fitting pieces together and then creating a mirror image.*	What accommodations could I include in this phase to make learning more accessible? *Tactile puzzles (tangrams)* *Use of multiple senses* *Cooperative learning* *The activity is hands-on.*	Student to Student *Students work in groups of two to four.* Student to Teacher *Students may ask for clarification but are allowed to discuss without teacher intervention.*
What tools and materials are needed for this activity? *Tangrams, paper, and ruler*	What questions might students raise? *How do I know if it is a mirror image?*	Teacher to Student *The teacher is a facilitator in this phase.*
What prior knowledge do I want to activate? *Informal understanding of symmetry*	*Why don't my two halves look the same? [May occur if student does not trace the entire figure correctly]*	Facilitation Questions *Describe how you recreated your partner's design.*
What nonconceptual vocabulary do I need to preteach? *Join* *Mirror image*		*Are the tangram pieces on one side of the ruler in exactly the same position as the tangram pieces on the other side of the ruler? Why or why not?*

Remember, the Engage phase is used to create interest and make connections to prior knowledge. Suspend judgment while asking probing questions to find out what the student already knows.

Explore

The Explore portion of the lesson provides the student with an opportunity to be actively involved in the exploration of the key mathematical concepts addressed in the lesson and to probe, inquire, and question. The role of the teacher is to observe and listen to students as they interact with each other. This part of the lesson is designed for groups of two to four students.

1. Distribute one copy of the Reflection Path, Rotation Path, and Translation Path Activity Cards, and a set of Transformation Paths Shapes to each pair of students.

2. Prompt the students to move the appropriate shape in numerical order along the path of shapes. Prompt the students to select a shape that matches the shape pictured on the Reflection Path Activity Card.

3. Prompt the students to move the shape along the Reflection Path in the order given.

4. Prompt the students to repeat steps one and two for the Rotation Path and Translation Path Activity Cards.

All children can learn and succeed but not the same day in the same way.

—James Spady

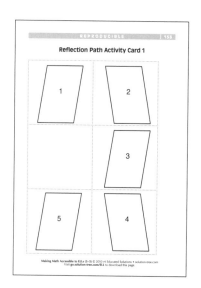

REPRODUCIBLE   155

Reflection Path Activity Card 1

1   2

3

5   4

Making Math Accessible to ELLs (3–5) © 2010 r4 Educated Solutions • solution-tree.com
Visit go.solution-tree.com/ELL to download this page

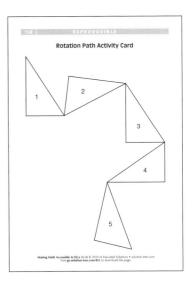

Rotation Path Activity Card

Facilitation Questions: Explore Phase

How did you move the shape on each step of the path?
Answers may vary. Possible answers include: I had to flip it over. I had to turn it around to fit.

Were you able to move the shape from one step to another without picking it up? Why or why not?
Answers may vary. Possible answers include: Reflections—no; rotations and translations—yes.

Did you move the piece vertically/horizontally for each step?
Answers may vary.

Table 5.4 shows how the Explore phase of this lesson supports students in understanding, participating, and communicating.

Table 5.4: Debriefing the Explore Phase of a 5E Lesson

Content Objective	Language Objective	Study/Metacognitive Objective
Understanding	*Participating*	*Communicating*
What concept(s) will students explore? *Reflections* *Rotations* *Translations* What activity will I use to encourage students to explore the concept(s)? *Students will physically move shapes in ways to help them identify translations, rotations, and reflections.* What tools or materials will allow students to become directly involved in exploring the concept(s)? *Paper cutouts of shapes* *Activity cards with paths upon which to move the shapes to represent translations, rotations, and reflections* What vocabulary and symbols do students need to understand for this phase? *Reflection (flip or mirror image)* *Rotation (turn)* *Translation (slide)* *Transformation* *Vertically* *Horizontally*	What accommodations could I include in this phase to make learning more accessible? *Students complete hands-on activities with pictures.* *Cooperative learning* *Peer tutors (if needed)* What questions might students raise? *Where do I start?* *Which way do I go first?* *What does "vertically" [or "horizontally"] mean?*	Student to Student *Students work in groups of two to four.* Student to Teacher *Students may ask for clarification but are allowed to explore with the group.* Teacher to Student *The teacher is a facilitator in this phase.* Facilitation Questions *How did you move the shape on each step of the path?* *Were you able to move the shape from one step to another without picking it up? Why or why not?* *Did you move the piece vertically/ horizontally for each step?*

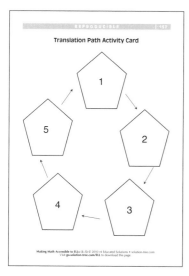

In the Explore phase, students work together, and the teacher asks facilitation questions. Allow time for students to problem solve through tasks. Listen to what students say as they interact.

Explain

The Explain phase of the lesson is directed by the teacher to allow students to formalize their understanding of the mathematics objectives addressed in the lesson.

1. Distribute a Transformation Path Activity Card and the Transformation Path Directions to each student.

2. Display the Transformation Path Activity Card on an overhead projector.

3. Prompt the students to move their shapes to complete step one on the activity card.

4. Model the movement of step one on the overhead.

5. Prompt the students to use a mirror to create a reflection of the first shape.

6. Prompt the students to record their answers on the Transformation Path Directions.

7. Prompt the students to move their shapes to complete step two. (Model on the overhead.)

8. Prompt the students to record their answers on the Transformation Path Directions.

> All children can learn and succeed but not the same day in the same way
>
> —James Spady

Facilitation Questions: Explain Phase

How can you describe how your piece moved to complete step one?
It flipped over.

Were you able to complete step one without picking up your shape? Why or why not?
No.

Does the image in the mirror look like the shape after completing step one?
Yes.

What do we call an image in a mirror?
Reflection

What do you think we call the new position of the shape after we moved it for step one?
Reflection

Can you describe how your piece moved to complete step two?
Answers may vary.

What is another word for *turn*?
Answers may vary. Guide students to the word rotate.

What do you think we call the new position of the shape after we moved it for step two?
Rotation

9. Explain to the students that this is the point of rotation.

10. Prompt the students to label the point of rotation on their Transformation Path Activity Card.

11. Prompt the students to move their shapes to complete step three. (Model on the overhead.)

12. Explain to the students that sliding the shape to a new position without rotating/turning or reflecting/flipping it represents a *translation*.

13. Prompt the students to record their answers on the Transformation Path Directions.

14. Prompt the students to complete the remaining steps on the Transformation Path Activity Card and record their findings on the Transformation Path Directions.

15. Prompt the students to create a transformation path of their own on another sheet of paper and share with their partner.

16. Prompt the students to work through their partner's transformation path, describing each transformation that occurs as they move the shape along the path.

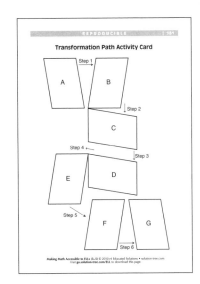

Transformation Path Activity Card

Facilitation Questions: Explain Phase

When you rotated your shape, was there any part of the shape that stayed in the same location? If so, which part?
Yes. One corner of the shape stayed in the same location.

How could you describe how your shape moved to complete step three?
Answers may vary. Possible answers include: I had to slide it down to a new position.

Did your shape rotate when you moved it?
No.

Did you have to flip your shape over in order to complete step three?
No.

Did you have to pick it up to move it to complete step three?
No.

How could you describe how your shape moved to complete step four? Five? Six? Did your shape rotate when you moved it?
Answers may vary. Possible answers include: No, my shape didn't rotate.

Did you have to flip your shape over in order to complete step four? Five? Six?
No (steps four and five).

Yes (step six).

Did you have to pick it up to move it to complete step four? Five? Six?
No (steps four and five).

Yes (step six).

How do you know that you have matched the cards correctly?
Answers may vary.

17. Distribute one set of the Transformation Match-Up Cards to each pair of students.

18. Prompt the students to match each word with the appropriate graphical representation for that word.

Table 5.5 shows how the Explain phase of this lesson supports students in understanding, participating, and communicating.

In the Explain phase, help students formalize what they have explored as conceptual vocabulary. Be sure to correct any misconceptions.

Table 5.5: Debriefing the Explain Phase of a 5E Lesson

Content Objective	Language Objective	Study/Metacognitive Objective
Understanding	*Participating*	*Communicating*
What misconceptions do I anticipate that may need to be corrected? *Students may not associate the concrete/kinetic activity with the vocabulary associated with it.* *Students may not transfer the concrete/kinetic experience to pictorial models.* How will I develop conceptual vocabulary? *By making strong associations between the kinetic experience and the vocabulary associated with the movement.* What connections are essential for the student to understand? *How the shapes move to create a reflection, rotation, or translation* *Differences among the transformations* What algorithms (computational procedures) are connected to the concept? *Use of a scale factor*	What accommodations could I include in this phase to make learning more accessible? *Hands-on activities allow students to try ideas before committing them to pencil and paper.* *Flexible grouping* *Peer tutors (if needed)* What questions might students raise? *How can I tell if it is a reflection (flip) or a rotation (turn)?* *Can I slide it and then flip it over? Why not? [This concept will be reinforced in the Elaborate phase when students investigate lines of symmetry.]*	Student to Student *Students explain possible answers to each other.* Student to Teacher *Students show how they solved the problem, perhaps by pointing, drawing, and demonstrating.* Teacher to Student *The teacher debriefs activities using facilitating questions.* *The teacher encourages students to examine alternative methods of solving problems.* Facilitation Questions *How can you describe how your piece moved to complete step one?* *Were you able to complete step one without picking up your shape? Why or why not?* *Does the image in the mirror look like the shape after completing step one?* *What do we call an image in a mirror?* *What do you think we call the new position of the shape after we moved it for step one?* *Can you describe how your piece moved to complete step two?* *What is another word for* turn? *What do you think we call the new position of the shape after we moved it for step two?*

Content Objective	Language Objective	Study/Metacognitive Objective
Understanding	*Participating*	*Communicating*
What new vocabulary is introduced? Reinforce: *Reflection* *Rotation* *Translation* *Transformation*		*When you rotated your shape, was there any part of the shape that stayed in the same location? If so, which part?*
		How could you describe how your shape moved to complete step three?
		Did your shape rotate when you moved it?
		Did you have to flip your shape over in order to complete step three?
		Did you have to pick it up to move it to complete step three?
		How could you describe how your shape moved to complete step four? Five? Six? Did your shape rotate when you moved it?
		Did you have to flip your shape over in order to complete step four? Five? Six?
		Did you have to pick it up to move it to complete step four? Five? Six?
		How do you know that you have matched the cards correctly?

Elaborate

The Elaborate phase of the lesson provides an opportunity for the student to apply the concepts of the mathematics objectives within a new situation. In this lesson, students will explore the concept of symmetry. This part of the lesson is designed for groups of three to four students.

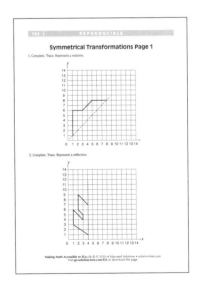

1. Distribute the Symmetrical Transformations reproducibles and several sheets of patty paper or tracing paper to each student.

2. Prompt the students to fold the patty paper in half twice and cut the patty paper into four squares (see fig. 5.2).

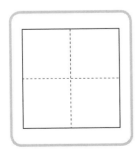

Figure 5.2: Folded patty paper.

3. Prompt the students to complete the first three drawings on the Symmetrical Transformations reproducibles using the dashed line as a line of symmetry.

4. Prompt the students to trace each completed figure on a piece of patty paper.

5. Prompt the students to check for accuracy by folding the patty paper figure in half along its line of symmetry to see if the halves of the drawing are mirror images of each other.

6. Prompt the students to glue the patty paper figure in a new position on the grid to represent the transformation indicated.

7. Prompt the students to create their own symmetrical drawing on the last grid, trace it on patty paper, and move it to a new position on the grid to represent the transformation of their choice.

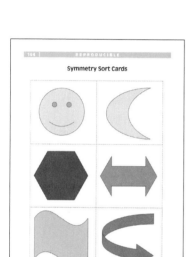

Facilitation Questions: Elaborate Phase

Answers to all may vary.

What strategy did you use for drawing the figures?

If you did not draw the other half of the figure accurately, how could you use the patty paper to help you?

How did you decide upon the new position in which to glue your patty paper figure?

Which transformation is represented by the position of your traced figure? How do you know?

---

8. Distribute the Symmetry Sort Cards and Symmetry Sort Mat to each pair of students.

9. Prompt the students to determine the number of lines of symmetry that each shape has.

10. Prompt the students to sort the Symmetry Sort Cards according to the number of lines of symmetry contained, placing the cards in the appropriate columns on the Symmetry Sort Mat.

11. Allow the students to use patty paper to trace the figures, fold them, and confirm their answers.

12. Distribute the Vocabulary Organizer reproducible to each student.

13. Prompt the students to complete the vocabulary organizers in groups of three and then share their conclusions in a Bonded Brains activity (see fig. 5.3).

14. As the students debrief with each group, encourage the students to make revisions to their vocabulary organizers when appropriate.

15. Beginning level students may use the Transformation Match-Up Cards.

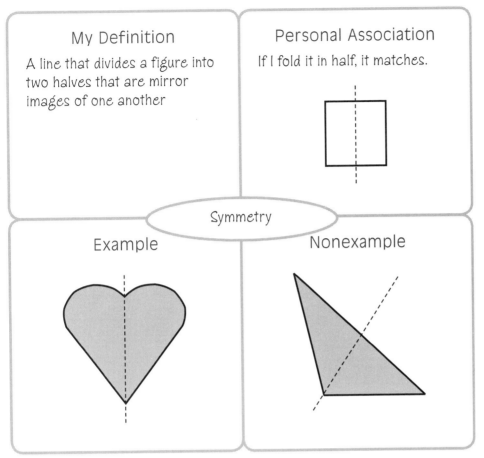

My Definition

A line that divides a figure into two halves that are mirror images of one another

Personal Association

If I fold it in half, it matches.

Symmetry

Example

Nonexample

Figure 5.3: Sample vocabulary organizer for *symmetry*.

Facilitation Questions: Elaborate Phase

Answers to all may vary.

How did your responses on your vocabulary organizers differ from other students' responses? How were they the same?

Did you revise any of the responses on your vocabulary organizers based on conversations that you had with other students? If so, what revisions did you make?

Table 5.6 (page 104) shows how the Elaborate phase of this lesson supports students in understanding, participating, and communicating.

In the Elaborate phase, encourage students to use formal labels and definitions that were developed earlier in the lesson. Provide opportunities for students to discover the benefit of sharing explanations with each other.

Table 5.6: Debriefing the Elaborate Phase of a 5E Lesson

Content Objective	Language Objective	Study/Metacognitive Objective
Understanding	*Participating*	*Communicating*
What activity will I use to expand or elaborate on the concept(s)? *Students will explore symmetry.*	What accommodations could I include in this phase to make learning more accessible? *The Vocabulary Organizer and Vocabulary Match-Up Cards for beginning students are hands-on as well as visual.*	Student to Student *Students will work in flexible groups.*
What tools or materials are needed for this activity? *Patty paper or tracing paper*	*Flexible grouping*	Student to Teacher *The teacher gives opportunities not only for verbal and written communication, but also for nonverbal communication such as drawing, pointing, and demonstrating.*
Scissors	*Peer tutors (if needed)*	Teacher to Student *The teacher acts as facilitator.*
What new vocabulary will students need for this phase of the lesson? *Symmetry*	What questions might students raise? *How can I be sure I have identified a line of symmetry?*	Facilitation Questions *What strategy did you use for drawing the figures?*
How will I encourage the use of vocabulary? *It is revisited and further developed in the extension of the concept.*	*Can there be more than one line of symmetry?*	*If you did not draw the other half of the figure accurately, how could you use the patty paper to help you?*
What concepts and processes must students understand to be successful with this phase of the lesson? *Lines of symmetry*	*What is the most lines of symmetry a figure can have?*	*How did you decide upon the new position in which to glue your patty paper figure?*
How (if at all) must the algorithms (computational procedures) be applied? *Arithmetic operations are not the focus of this phase of the lesson.*		*Which transformation is represented by the position of your traced figure? How do you know?*
		How did your responses on your Vocabulary Organizer differ from other students' responses? How were they the same?
		Did you revise any of the responses on your Vocabulary Organizer based on conversations that you had with other students? If so, what revisions did you make?

Evaluate

The Evaluate phase of the lesson provides the student an opportunity to demonstrate his or her understanding of the mathematics objectives addressed in the lesson.

1. Distribute the Performance Assessment reproducible to each student.

2. Prompt the students to use the six pattern blocks to create a design.

3. Prompt the students to trace their design on the grid provided.

4. Prompt the students to show a translation of their design using the pattern blocks, trace the design in its new position, and shade or color the translated design to distinguish it from the original design (see fig. 5.4).

5. Prompt the students to explain their thinking as they complete the activity.

Create a design using the pattern blocks shown below and record it on the grid provided. Show a translation of your design. Record the translation of your design on the grid, and shade the translated design. Explain your thinking.

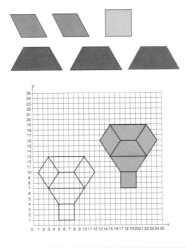

Figure 5.4: Sample Performance Assessment for lesson.

HOT TIP!

Use the following verbs to guide you in creating appropriate assessments. Introduce boldfaced words at the indicated proficiency level.

Assessment Verbs				
Beginning	Early Intermediate	Intermediate	Advanced	Proficient
Choose	Choose	Choose	Choose	Choose
Draw	Draw	Draw	Draw	Draw
Point	Point	Point	Point	Point
Label	Label	Label	Label	Label
Select	Select	Select	Select	Select
	Group	Group	Group	Group
	List	List	List	List
	Name	Name	Name	Name
		Answer	Answer	Answer
		Compare	Compare	Compare
		Contrast	Contrast	Contrast
		Define	Define	Define
		Describe	Describe	Describe
		Explain	Explain	Explain
			Analyze	Analyze
			Evaluate	Evaluate
			Justify	Justify

Table 5.7 shows how the Evaluate phase of this lesson supports students in understanding, participating, and communicating.

Table 5.7: Debriefing the Evaluate Phase of a 5E Lesson

Content Objective	Language Objective	Study/Metacognitive Objective
Understanding	*Participating*	*Communicating*
What activity will I use to assess learning? *A performance assessment* What concept(s) will I assess? *Translations, rotations, symmetry, and reflections* What additional skills must the students have to complete this phase successfully? *None* What tools and materials will students need to complete the task? *Pattern blocks*	What accommodations could I include in this phase to make learning more accessible? *Model the task.* *Allow students to work in pairs or small groups.* What questions might students raise? *Do I have to use all the pattern block pieces?* *Does it matter which direction I translate my design?*	Student to Student *Students should work independently.* Student to Teacher *Students could ask teacher for clarification of expectations.* Teacher to Student *The teacher asks facilitation questions as needed.*

It is appropriate for students to complete performance assessments in small groups or as a class as the assessments are phased in. Only after students have worked performance assessments in groups and have been provided opportunities for teacher and peer feedback should they be expected to work performance assessments independently. It is important to maintain a nurturing environment, establish support, and value each student on a continuing basis.

Table 5.8 shows how this 5E lesson meets the needs of English language learners.

Table 5.8: Meeting the Needs of ELLs

Affective Needs	Linguistic Needs	Cognitive Needs
• Flexible grouping establishes support. • Use peer tutors if needed. • Students can help each other. • Concrete objects enhance learning, make the concept easier to understand, and lower student stress. • Teacher is the facilitator, not "the sage on the stage."	• Student lesson is in a sans-serif font, such as Arial or Helvetica. • Manipulatives, visuals, graphics, and simplified language make the concept more accessible. • Activity cards and organizers provide nonverbal learning opportunities. • Charts and tables provide nonverbal and reduced-verbal learning opportunities. • Student-to-student, student-to-teacher, and teacher-to-student dialogue provide opportunities for language enrichment. • Vocabulary organizers make terminology more accessible. • Students can respond in nonverbal and reduced-verbal ways.	• The Engage portion activates prior knowledge. • The tangrams stimulate interest. • Comparing and contrasting stimulates long-term memory. • Group work allows students to learn from each other. • Hands-on activities make learning the concept more efficient. • Assessment measures mathematical proficiency, not reading proficiency, by providing more than one way to find the answer. • Facilitation questions build understanding by scaffolding the content. • Opportunities for the student to think about his or her own thinking increases metacognitive skills.

BIG IDEAS

- The 5E model provides a practical vehicle for implementing the components of an effective lesson.

- The five phases of the 5E model are:

  1. **Engage**—Designed to interest students in the problem and to make connections between past and present learning

  2. **Explore**—Designed to provide the opportunity for students to become directly involved with the key concepts with the teacher observing and listening to students as they interact with each other

  3. **Explain**—Designed for the teacher to act as a facilitator to formalize understanding, correct any misconceptions, and provide further meaning or information

  4. **Elaborate**—Designed to allow students to extend and expand what they have learned in the first three phases

  5. **Evaluate**—Designed to allow the teacher to determine whether the learner has reached the desired level of understanding the key ideas and concepts

Points to Ponder

How might you begin to implement 5E lessons in your classroom?

When might be a "comfortable" place in your curriculum to try a 5E lesson?

How might you adapt traditional lessons to incorporate some of the benefits to students the 5E model provides?

6

Adapting a Traditional Textbook Lesson

A small part of even the most reluctant student wants to learn.

—Anonymous

Traditional textbook lessons present several concerns. The lesson format generally lends itself to teacher-centered instruction instead of student-centered instruction. The content of standard textbook lessons rarely includes examples and problems with the cognitive rigor necessary to prepare students for success—whether success is measured by standardized tests or readiness for post–high school education. Such lessons seldom include strategies for building common background, developing vocabulary, providing comprehensibility, and solving authentic problems in an atmosphere ripe for interaction. Therefore, teachers often face the challenge of adapting traditional lessons to meet the needs of English language learners.

Figure 6.1 (pages 110–111) represents what a teacher might see in a traditional textbook lesson in which students will explore line graphs.

Tell me and I'll forget, show me and I may remember, involve me and I'll understand.

—Chinese proverb

Chapter 6.3
Using Line Graphs

What You Will Learn
To use line graphs to analyze data

Why It Is Important to Learn
We all deal with large amounts of data. Line graphs help us organize information in picture form to make the information easier to interpret.

Vocabulary to Remember
- Line graph
- Scale
- Interval
- Vertical axis
- Horizontal axis

Introduction
What is a line graph? Where have you seen a line graph before?

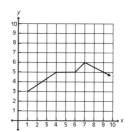

Lesson

A. A line graph can be used to show how data changes over time.

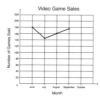

What does the horizontal axis represent? *Months*

What does the vertical axis represent? *Number of games sold*

During which two months were the most games sold? *June and September*

Between which two months did the greatest decrease in sales occur? *Between June and July*

Over how many months was the number of sales recorded? *4 months*

The horizontal axis is the *x*-**axis**.

The vertical axis is the *y*-**axis**.

The period of time over which the data is displayed is the **interval**.

B. Consider the information in the following table.

Francis Elementary Enrollment	
Month	Number of Students
August	425
September	435
October	442
November	438
December	427

Represent the data as a line graph.

Step 1: Detemine the intervals.
Step 2: Label the axes.
Step 3: Plot the data points.
Step 4: Since the data represents change over time, connect the data points.

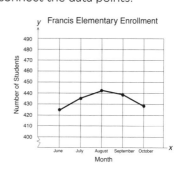

Check for Understanding

Use the folowing line graph to answer Questions 1–3.

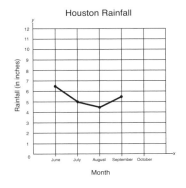

Houston Rainfall

1. What does the *x*-axis represent? *The months the rainfall occurred*

2. How much rain fell in July? *5 inches*

3. About how much difference was there in the amount of rainfall between August and September? *An increase of about 1 inch*

Practice

Use the line graph to answer Questions 4–6.

72

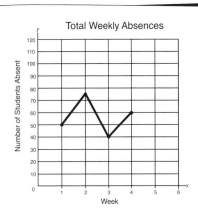

Total Weekly Absences

4. What do the numbers on the *y*-axis represent? *The number of students absent*

5. What intervals were used? *Weeks*

6. Between which two weeks did the number of students absent increase the most? *Between weeks one and two, and between weeks three and four*

73

7. Graph the data in the following table. Be sure to label your axes.

Overdue Jenson Library Books	
Month	**Number of Overdue Books**
January	75
February	60
March	55
April	57
May	80
June	92

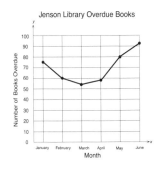

Jenson Library Overdue Books

74

Challenge

8. About how long did Diane practice piano in hours and minutes? *About 3 hours and 20 minutes*

Diane's Daily Piano Practice

75

Figure 6.1: Sample textbook lesson on line graphs.

The Stages of Implementation

We have included a possible adaptation of the traditional textbook lesson in figure 6.1 for all five phases of the 5E model. However, we encourage you to begin adapting lessons in stages. Study the chart in table 6.1 to determine at which stage you would place yourself. If you try to start at stage five and are used to students sitting in rows and using a standard textbook as your curriculum (which may have been a district or campus expectation), you will set yourself up for failure by beginning at that stage. This self-evaluation is an important step in adapting lessons to the 5E model.

Table 6.1: Stages of 5E Implementation

Stage One	Stage Two	Stage Three	Stage Four	Stage Five
I'm really comfortable with directly teaching the material by working at the overhead and having students follow my lead. I use the ancillaries provided with the textbook if I need additional materials.	I occasionally have students work with a partner or small group on an activity or project. I also sometimes have them use tools such as grid paper, patty paper, color tiles, and base ten blocks. I look for materials from outside resources to enhance instruction.	I like to have a balance of group and independent work. I am comfortable using a variety of tools and frequently use materials other than the textbook.	I frequently have my students work in groups and am comfortable managing an interactive classroom. I believe it is important for students to work and talk together. I look for activities that are challenging and require students to think a step beyond the lesson objective.	I create many of my own materials and mainly use the textbook as a resource for practice problems. My students routinely work in cooperative groups. I am comfortable with lots of activity in the classroom and enjoy trying innovative things.
Focus on the Engage and Explain phases.	Focus on the Engage and Explain phases.	Focus on the Explore phase.	Focus on the Elaborate phase.	Put it all together to create a 5E lesson.

Stage One

Traditional textbook lessons will not constitute an entire 5E lesson. Decide if the lesson includes an appropriate Engage component. If it does not include an activity to stimulate student interest and to activate prior knowledge, think about what tools you have used or would like to use to set the stage for the lesson. If you want students to learn about line graphs, possible tools might include coordinate grid paper, patty paper, or geoboards.

In the Explain phase of the lesson, focus on how to debrief the Explore part of the lesson. You may have used the textbook examples and guided-practice problems for exploration. Asking questions that give insight into student processing and providing the opportunity to correct any misconceptions will enhance retention and provide a strong foundation for exploring the concept at greater depth and complexity. Reviewing the facilitation questions in chapter 5 may be helpful in the continuing journey to strengthen your questioning strategies. Listening to student responses and asking follow-up questions that build understanding will require planning and practice, but will result in accelerated learning.

Stage Two

The quality of instruction in the Explore phase of the lesson is one of the most powerful ways to accelerate language and mathematical proficiency. The opportunity is ripe in the Explore phase to link concrete representations to abstract concepts. By carefully evaluating available tools and choosing the most effective ones to encourage student interaction, you can bring a forgettable traditional textbook lesson to life for your students.

Your challenge is not only to decide which tool would be most effective, but also to manage a student-centered, interactive classroom. Activities must be well planned, and expected behaviors must be overtly taught and reinforced throughout the year. Start small, perhaps having students work with a partner for five minutes on a specific task. As students become accustomed to expectations and routines, and as you feel more comfortable with student-centered instruction, you may expand the size of the groups to three or four students and increase the length of time devoted to more complex tasks.

Stage Three

Appropriately assessing student progress is critical in determining student strengths, weaknesses, and possible misconceptions. Whether you are using selected-response items or a performance assessment, assessments should mirror instruction, occur continuously, and provide information about the student's level of understanding. Selected-response items—whether multiple-choice, true/false, matching, or fill-in-the-blank—can provide information about mastery of the concept as well as pinpoint areas of deficiency. Performance assessments allow students to demonstrate their understanding by solving a task in one of several possible ways. As discussed earlier, performance assessments should be phased in, and students can benefit from hearing and seeing other students' strategies for solving the same problem.

Stage Four

The Elaborate phase of the lesson allows for an expanded or extended look at the lesson concepts. Again, the selection of appropriate tools is important, as is providing affective, linguistic, and cognitive supports so students are likely to succeed. This phase of the 5E model is often the answer to the question, How do I get students to think? Evidence of increased student thinking is not generally instantaneous but compounds with routine implementation of the 5E model.

Stage Five

Frequently seeking out resources that expand student thinking and creating your own materials are indicators that you know there are more effective means to provide instruction than to teach a traditional textbook lesson using a teacher-centered instructional model. The advantage of using the 5E model is that it provides a research-based framework for developing effective materials, deciding the most efficient place in the lesson to include the materials, and ensuring a student-centered classroom.

The shell must break before the bird can fly.

—Lord Alfred Tennyson

Planning an Adapted Lesson

When you ask yourself the following questions about previously developed activities or when you consider new activities, it becomes easier to determine whether an activity or task serves the intended purpose:

- Does the activity interest students in the problem and make connections between past and present learning? (Engage)

- Does the activity provide the opportunity for students to become directly involved in the key concepts of the lesson by interacting with each other and the activity? (Explore)

- Retention and use of math vocabulary are more meaningful after students have had a direct experience with the concept. Is there opportunity to formalize the concepts and vocabulary? Is there opportunity for students to draw conclusions and communicate them to each other and to you, the teacher? (Explain)

- Does the activity allow students to extend and expand what they learned in the first three stages? (Elaborate)

- Does the assessment allow you to determine whether the learner has reached the desired level of understanding of the key ideas and concepts? (Evaluate)

Since we know the 5E model is effective in meeting our students' needs, we will use the 5E lesson plan template to organize our thoughts (see appendix F, page 173, for a template). The adaptation of the traditional textbook lesson to the 5E model need not be a daunting task. Table 6.2 expresses what may be in fact a short thought process.

Table 6.2: 5E Lesson Plan for Investigating Line Graphs

Content Objective	Language Objectives	Study/Metacognitive Objective
Students will display data in line graphs and interpret line graphs.	<ul><li>Beginning students will demonstrate understanding of key vocabulary using manipulatives and drawings.</li><li>Early intermediate students will use phrases and short sentences to communicate understanding, both verbally and in writing.</li><li>Intermediate students will use phrases and short sentences to communicate understanding, both verbally and in writing.</li><li>Advanced students will use complete sentences to communicate understanding, both verbally and in writing.</li><li>Proficient students will use complete sentences with descriptive language to communicate understanding, both verbally and in writing.</li></ul>	Students will justify solutions, verbally or nonverbally, depending on proficiency level.

Materials	Preparation
For each group of two to four students: • Example/Nonexample Situation Cards in a resealable bag • Example/Nonexample Sorting Mat • Matching Tables and Graphs Cards in a resealable bag • Large resealable bags containing 25 index cards and a length of string approximately 4 yards long • Floor Graph Labels • Floor Graph Title • Floor Graph Numbers (*x*-axis) • Floor Graph Numbers (*y*-axis) *For each student:* • 10" x 10" piece of one-inch grid paper • Matching Tables and Graphs handout • Daily Temperatures performance assessment *For the teacher:* • Transparencies or slides of Weekly Reading Problem, Weekly Reading Table, and Sample Line Graphs • Data Table Cards (2 sets) • Floor Graph Labels • Floor Graph Title • Floor Graph Numbers (*x*-axis) • Floor Graph Numbers (*y*-axis) • String	1. Prepare the transparencies. 2. Sort cards into bags. 3. Copy student handouts. 4. Use masking tape to create a large grid on the floor. Make sure the grid is big enough (approximately 10' x 10') for students to stand on it to represent the data points of a line graph. 5. Read and select Facilitation Questions appropriate for students' needs.

Engage

The Engage portion of the lesson is designed to interest students in investigating graphing data. The adaptation of the traditional textbook lesson to the 5E model need not be a daunting task. Table 6.3 expresses what may be in fact a short thought process: a teacher's plan for the Engage phase of this adapted textbook lesson.

Table 6.3: The Engage Phase of an Adapted Lesson

Content Objective	Language Objective	Study/Metacognitive Objective
Understanding	*Participating*	*Communicating*
What activity will I use to stimulate curiosity and activate prior knowledge? *Weekly Reading Problem* What tools and materials are needed for this activity? *Sets of cards to create a large graph on the floor* What prior knowledge do I want to activate? *Making lists, tables, and graphs*	What accommodations could I include in this phase to make learning more accessible? *Creating the human line graph is an appropriate accommodation.* *I will hold books or point to weeks on calendar for beginning level students, if necessary.* *Students will act out finding the correct position on the floor grid.* What questions might students raise? *Do I move across or up first?*	Student to Student *Students will work together and discuss their strategies.* Student to Teacher *Students can ask questions about finding their position.* Teacher to Student *I will set the stage for activity, monitor student groups, and check student work.* Facilitation Questions *How could we organize the information from this problem so that it is easier to interpret?*

continued on next page→

Content Objective	Language Objective	Study/Metacognitive Objective
Understanding	*Participating*	*Communicating*
What nonconceptual vocabulary do I need to preteach? *Data* *Table*	*How do you know which label to use for the x-axis and which to use for the y-axis?*	*How could you describe what the information would look like if we put it in a table?*
		What is another way that we could represent the information?
		How did I know where to position the students on the graph?
		What could we add to the graph to ensure that the students are placed correctly?
		Are there any other pieces of information from the table that are missing from our floor graph?
		What piece of information from the table is being represented by (name of student)?
		How does the string help us interpret the information?
		What are some conclusions that we can make by looking at the graphical representation of the information from the weekly reading problem?

1. The teacher displayed the Weekly Reading Problem form on an overhead and prompted the students to brainstorm ways to represent the information in the problem.

2. Next, the teacher displayed the Weekly Reading Table form on an overhead and had the students work as a group to finish filling in the table with the information from the problem (see fig. 6.2).

3. She placed the Floor Graph Numbers y-axis next to the appropriate lines on the y-axis of the floor graph and placed the Floor Graph Numbers x-axis next to the appropriate lines on the x-axis of the floor graph.

4. She placed the Floor Graph Labels and Floor Graph Title in the appropriate position on the floor graph (see fig. 6.3).

5. The teacher positioned students on the floor graph to represent the data points represented in the table.

6. To demonstrate a line graph, the teacher used a long piece of string to connect the data points (students).

Weekly Reading Problem Transparency

Mary Ann kept a record of the number of library books she read each week. The first week she read 6 books. The second week she read 4 books. The third week she read 5 books. The fourth week she read 8 books. The fifth week she read 6 books.

How can we represent the information in this problem?

Weekly Reading Table	
Week	*Number of Books Read*
1	6
2	

Figure 6.2: Sample transparency for adapted lesson.

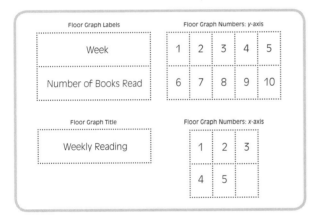

Figure 6.3: Sample tools for adapted lesson.

Facilitation Questions: Engage Phase

How could we organize the information from this problem so that it is easier to interpret?
Answers varied and included: We could make a list, table, or graph.

How could you describe what the information would look like if we put it in a table?
Answers varied and included: The table would have columns, rows, headings, and a title.

What is another way that we could represent the information?
Answers varied. The teacher guided students to graphs.

How did I know where to position the students on the graph?
Answers varied and included: The number of lines that corresponds with the number of books read

continued on next page→

What could we add to the graph to ensure that the students are placed correctly?
Answers varied and included: We could number the y-axis with the number of books read. We could number the x-axis with the week numbers.

Are there any other pieces of information from the table that are missing from our floor graph?
Answers varied. The teacher guided students to observe that the axis labels and graph title are missing.

What piece of information from the table is being represented by (name of student)?
Answers varied.

How does the string help us interpret the information?
Answers varied and included: It shows when the numbers go up and down.

What are some conclusions that we can make by looking at the graphical representation of the information from the weekly reading problem?
Answers varied and included: Mary Ann read more books during the fourth week than during any other week.

Explore

The Explore portion of the lesson provides students with an opportunity to be actively involved in the exploration of the key mathematical concepts addressed in the lesson and to probe, inquire, and question.

Table 6.4 shows the teacher's plan for the Explore phase of our adapted textbook lesson.

Table 6.4: The Explore Phase of an Adapted Lesson

Content Objective	Language Objective	Study/Metacognitive Objective
Understanding	*Participating*	*Communicating*
What concept(s) will students explore? *Creating a line graph from data contained in a table, using examples in a textbook lesson for context*	What accommodations could I include in this phase to make learning more accessible? *Using the tools and materials and working in groups provide appropriate accommodations.*	Student to Student *Students will still be in their groups.*
What activity will I use to encourage students to explore the concept(s)? *Students will use a Data Table Card on 10" x 10" grid paper to create group graphs.*	*I will include needed vocabulary on the word wall.* What questions might students raise? *Which column should I use to label the x-axis? the y-axis?*	Student to Teacher *Students will justify their answers.* Teacher to Student *I will facilitate the activity as necessary.*
What tools or materials will allow students to become directly involved in exploring the concept(s)? *10" x 10" grid paper* *Index cards*	*Should I start at zero?* *What do I do since there are not enough lines on the chart paper for each number to have its own line?*	Facilitation Questions *What is the lowest number that you will need to represent on your graph?* *What is the highest number that you will need to represent on your graph?* *How are you going to represent larger numbers on your graph, since you may not have enough lines to use on it?*

Content Objective	Language Objective	Study/Metacognitive Objective
Understanding	*Participating*	*Communicating*
String *Data Table Card* What vocabulary and symbols do students need to understand for this phase? X-*axis* Y-*axis* *Interval* *Range*		*What did we use to represent the pieces of data on our floor graph?* *How did you determine what data to represent on the x-axis of your line graph?* *How did you decide how to number the y-axis of your line graph?* *How did you decide how to label the x-axis and y-axis?* *How did you decide on the title of your graph?* *How do the labels on the line graphs compare to the column headings on the tables of data that we used?* *How are the labels for the x-axis on all of the line graphs similar?*

1. The teacher distributed a 10" x 10" piece of one-inch grid paper, one Data Table Card (see fig. 6.4), and a bag with twenty-five index cards and a length of string approximately four yards long to each group of four students.

Data Table Cards

Francis Elementary Enrollment	
Month	*Number of Students*
August	425
September	435
October	442
November	438
December	427

Overdue Jenson Library Books	
Month	*Number of Overdue Books*
January	75
February	60
March	55
April	57
May	80
June	92

Bicycle Sales	
Week	*Number of Bicycles Sold*
1	5
2	7
3	4
4	6

Daily Television Viewing	
Day	*Number of Minutes*
Tuesday	30
Wednesday	60
Thursday	45
Friday	55

Figure 6.4: Sample handout for adapted lesson.

2. She prompted the students to use the one-inch grid paper to create a line graph that represented the information from the Data Table Card.

3. She prompted the students to include all of the components that were discussed in the Engage portion of the lesson and to make sure that the title, labels, and numbers of the table are represented on the line graph.

4. Students used the index cards from the bag to create labels that represented the title, axis labels, and intervals of their line graph.

5. Students used the index card labels and members of their group to represent the data points on their floor graph.

6. Each group of students represented the information from their Data Table Card on the floor graph.

Facilitation Questions: Explore Phase

What is the lowest number that you will need to represent on your graph?
Answers varied.

What is the highest number that you will need to represent on your graph?
Answers varied.

How are you going to represent larger numbers on your graph, since you may not have enough lines to use on it?
Answers varied and included: We may count by fives, twos, or hundreds.

What did we use to represent the pieces of data on our floor graph?
We used the students in our group.

How did you determine what data to represent on the *x*-axis of your line graph?
Answers varied. Note: When graphing change over time, units of time are most often represented on the x-axis.

How did you decide how to number the *y*-axis of your line graph?
Answers varied. Student responses addressed the range of the data, even though that terminology might not have been part of the students' vocabulary at this time.

How did you decide how to label the *x*-axis and *y*-axis?
Answers varied and included: I used the column headings from the table.

How did you decide on the title of your graph?
Answers varied and included: We picked a title that described the purpose of the line graph.

How do the labels on the line graphs compare to the column headings on the tables of data that we used?
The column headings and labels are the same.

How are the labels for the *x*-axis on all of the line graphs similar?
Answers may vary.

The teacher guided students to the realization that all of the labels on the x-axis of each graph represent some unit of time.

What we see depends mainly on what we look for.

—Sir John Lubbock

Remember that it is important for students to explore. The Explore phase of a 5E lesson is not intended to be directly taught. The role of the teacher in this phase is that of a facilitator. In setting expectations for working with tools that could potentially be misused, it is important to establish rules and overtly teach appropriate behavior for different settings, such as group work, independent work, and testing.

Explain

The Explain phase of the lesson is directed by the teacher to allow students to formalize their understanding of the mathematics objectives addressed in the lesson.

Table 6.5 (page 122) shows the teacher's plan for the Explain phase of our adapted textbook lesson.

Table 6.5: The Explain Phase of an Adapted Lesson

Content Objective	Language Objective	Study/Metacognitive Objective
Understanding	*Participating*	*Communicating*
What misconceptions do I anticipate that may need to be corrected? *Inappropriate intervals, reversing x-axis and y-axis and/or the x and y values*	What accommodations could I include in this phase to make learning more accessible? *I will add vocabulary to the word wall.*	**Student to Student** *I will encourage students to communicate with each other to facilitate understanding.*
Some students may think any data can be represented using a line graph. Use an example/nonexample activity to clarify any misconceptions.	*I will remind students that they may use the picture dictionaries and bilingual dictionaries in the classroom resource center.*	**Student to Teacher** *Students will answer facilitation questions using both verbal and nonverbal communication.*
How will I develop conceptual vocabulary? *Sample Line Graphs to formalize concepts and reinforce vocabulary*	What questions might students raise? *How do I know what interval to use?*	**Teacher to Student** *I will ask facilitation questions.*
What connections are essential for the student to understand? *We must label the axes for the data to make sense.*	*Can the values I use on my graph be different from other students' values?*	**Facilitation Questions** *What do you notice about this line graph that is similar to the line graph that your group produced?*
Determining the scale and interval may require counting by twos, fives, tens, and so on.		*Is there any part of this line graph that was not included on your line graph?*
Line graphs are used to represent data that change over time.		*What do you notice about the way the y-axis is numbered?*
What algorithms (computational procedures) are connected to the concept? *None*		*What are the scale, interval, and range of the data on each of the Sample Line Graphs?*
What vocabulary is introduced? *Same as Explore.*		*What is the scale on the line graph that your group created?*
		What is the interval on the line graph that your group created?
		What labels did you put on your line graph?
		How does the line graph that your group created show change over time?
		What unit of time was represented on your group's line graph?
		What changes were represented by the data on your line graph?
		What part of the graph shows the change over time?
		What is one example of a situation that you placed in the "Example" column of the mat? Why did you place it there?
		What is the unit of time described in that situation?
		What type of graph is best for representing change over time situations?
		What is an example of a situation that you placed in the "Nonexample" column of the mat?
		Would it be appropriate to represent this nonexample situation on a line graph? Why or why not?
		What type of graph might be appropriate for representing the nonexample situation?

1. The teacher displayed the Sample Line Graph transparencies (fig. 6.5) showing the graphs from the textbook examples. The font was changed to Arial (sans serif).

2. She used the facilitation questions to discuss the attributes of the line graph "Video Game Sales" and for the other Sample Line Graphs.

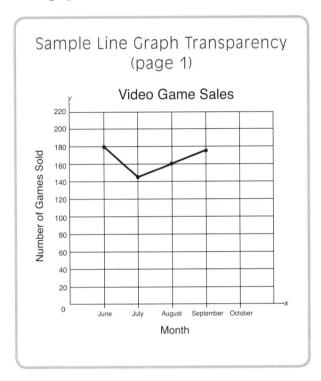

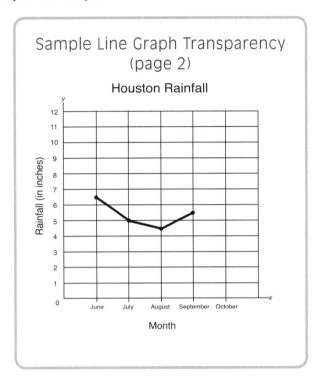

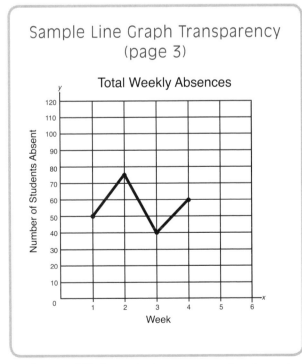

Figure 6.5: Sample transparencies for adapted lesson.

3. The teacher explained that specific pieces of information are called *data*, and that in order for the data to make sense, we have to label the axes on our graph.

4. She explained that on line graphs, the units of time are most often represented on the *x*-axis, the series of numbers on the *y*-axis is called the *scale*, and the distance between the numbers on the scale is called the *interval*.

Facilitation Questions: Explain Phase

What do you notice about this line graph that is similar to the line graph that your group produced?
Answers varied and included: We recorded the data about time on the x-axis. We used the same numbers.

Is there any part of this line graph that was not included on your line graph?
Answers varied.

What do you notice about the way the y-axis is numbered?
Answers varied and included: Some count by ones and others skip count.

Answers varied for the rest of the questions.

What are the scale, interval, and range of the data on each of the Sample Line Graphs?

What is the scale on the line graph that your group created?

What is the interval on the line graph that your group created?

What labels did you put on your line graph?

How does the line graph that your group created show change over time?

What unit of time was represented on your group's line graph?

What changes were represented by the data on your line graph?

---

5. The teacher explained that the difference between the largest piece of data and the smallest piece of data is called the *range* of the data, and that line graphs represent how something changes over a period of time.

6. She distributed one set of Example/Nonexample Situation Cards and one Example/Nonexample Sorting Mat to each pair of students (see figs. 6.6 and 6.7).

7. The teacher prompted the students to determine if the situation described on each card was an example of a situation that describes change over time.

8. Students placed the cards with examples of situations that described change over time in the "Example" column of the mat and cards that were not examples of situations describing change over time in the "Nonexamples" column of the mat.

Example and Nonexample Situation Cards

Card A

Joel recorded the attendance at the local skating rink for 5 days. On Monday, 150 people attended the skating rink. On Tuesday, 155 people attended the skating rink. On Wednesday, 165 people attended the rink. On Thursday, 180 people attended. On Friday and Saturday, 230 people attended each day.

Card B

Jameson Elementary School sold jelly beans for their spring fundraiser. Mrs. Marquette recorded her class's sales in the following table.

Week	Number of Bags Sold
1	45
2	27
3	36

Card C

Starting at 8:00 a.m., Marvin recorded the outside temperature every 4 hours until midnight.

Card D

Donte's compact disc collection contains 24 rock CDs, 19 classical ones, 7 R&B ones, and 2 country ones.

Card E

Madeleine surveyed students in her class to determine their favorite meals and recorded the information in the table below.

Favorite Meals	
Meal	*Number of Students*
Chicken	6
Ham	3
Pizza	12
Spaghetti	2

Card F

In the Marbles Elementary spring talent show, 12 acts are singers, 5 acts are dancers, 2 acts are baton twirlers, and 7 acts are instrumentalists.

Figure 6.6: Sample handout for adapted lesson.

Example and Nonexample Sorting Mat

Example	Nonexample

Figure 6.7: Sample handout for adapted lesson.

Facilitation Questions: Explain Phase

What part of the graph shows the change over time?
The line that connects the points on the graph

What is one example of a situation that you placed in the "Example" column of the mat? Why did you place it there?
Answers varied and included: I put Card B in the "Example" column because the table describes how the number of bags of jelly beans sold changed over a period of time (weeks).

What is the unit of time described in that situation?
Answers varied.

What type of graph is best for representing change over time situations?
Line graph

What is an example of a situation that you placed in the "Nonexample" column of the mat?
Answers varied and included: I put Card D in the "Nonexample" column because it does not represent a situation of some change happening over a period of time.

Would it be appropriate to represent this nonexample situation on a line graph? Why or why not?
Answers varied.

What type of graph might be appropriate for representing the nonexample situation?
Answers varied.

Elaborate

Table 6.6 shows the teacher's plan for the Elaborate phase of our adapted textbook lesson.

Table 6.6: The Elaborate Phase of an Adapted Lesson

Content Objective	Language Objective	Study/Metacognitive Objective
Understanding	*Participating*	*Communicating*
What activity will I use to expand or elaborate on the concept(s)? *Students will match tables and graphs.*	What accommodations could I include in this phase to make learning more accessible? *Students will work in pairs. The activity is tactile and visual and reinforces working with multiple representations of data.*	Student to Student *Students will discuss in pairs.*
What tools or materials are needed for this activity? *Matching Tables and Graphs Cards and Matching Tables and Graphs handouts from problems in textbook lessons and ancillaries*	*The card match activity provides accessibility by reducing the amount of pencil-and-paper work required.*	Student to Teacher *Students will justify their answers.* Teacher to Student *I will ask clarifying questions such as why or why not?*
What new vocabulary will students need for this phase of the lesson? *Range*	What questions might students raise? *How do I determine the range of the data?*	Facilitation Questions *How do you know that your tables are matched with the appropriate graphs?*
How will I encourage the use of vocabulary?		*How did you determine the title for your graph?* *How did you know how to label your graph? Why?*

Content Objective	Language Objective	Study/Metacognitive Objective
Understanding	*Participating*	*Communicating*
I will give opportunities to discuss and reinforce with a matching activity. What concepts and processes must students understand to be successful with this phase of the lesson? *Tabular and graphical representations of data* How (if at all) must the algorithms (computational procedures) be applied? *Arithmetic operations are not the focus of this phase of the lesson.*	*Do I need to include all the months or days of the week on the graph?*	*How did you find the range of the data on your line graph?* *Was the range of the set of data on your graph the same as the range of the set of data on your table? How do you know?*

1. The teacher distributed one set of the Matching Tables and Graphs Cards to each pair of students, and one copy of the Matching Tables and Graphs handout to each student (see figs. 6.8, 6.9, and 6.10, pages 128–129).

2. The teacher prompted the students to match each table on the Matching Tables and Graphs Cards with the line graph card that represents the data.

3. Students used the information given on the table and on the line graph to reproduce each line graph on the Matching Tables and Graphs handout.

4. Students added the appropriate labels and created a title for each line graph.

Facilitation Questions: Elaborate Phase

How do you know that your tables are matched with the appropriate graphs?
Answers varied.

How did you determine the title for your graph?
Answers varied and included: I used a title similar to the title of the table.

How did you know how to label your graph? Why?
Answers varied and included: I used the column headings from the table.

How did you find the range of the data on your line graph?
Answers varied and included: I subtracted the lowest number from the highest number.

Was the range of the set of data on your graph the same as the range of the set of data on your table? How do you know?
Answers varied and included: When I subtracted the lowest number from the highest number on the data table and the lowest number from the highest number on the graph, they were the same.

Matching Tables and Graphs Cards (page 1)

Francis Elementary Enrollment	
Month	*Number of Students*
August	425
September	435
October	442
November	438
December	427

Daily Plate Lunch Sales	
Day	*Number of Plate Lunches Sold*
Monday	270
Tuesday	340
Wednesday	300
Thursday	295
Friday	240

Overdue Jenson Library Books	
Month	*Number of Overdue Books*
January	75
February	60
March	55
April	57
May	80
June	92

Time Spent on Homework	
Day	*Number of Minutes*
Monday	65
Tuesday	60
Wednesday	25
Thursday	90
Friday	30

Figure 6.8: Sample handout for adapted lesson.

Since the concept is extended or expanded in the Elaborate phase of the lesson, it is appropriate to use different or additional tools. For example, use modified assessment items to create card-matching activities.

Matching Tables and Graphs Cards (page 2)

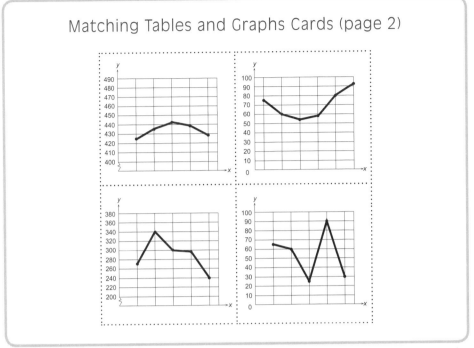

Figure 6.9: Sample handout for adapted lesson.

Matching Tables and Graphs

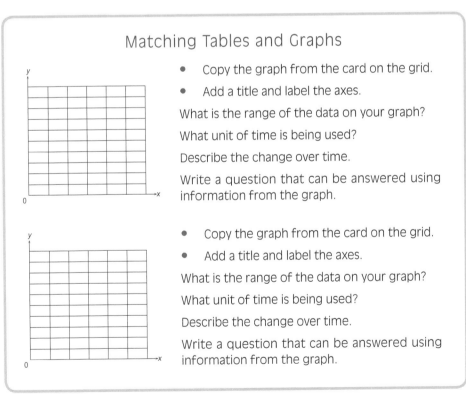

- Copy the graph from the card on the grid.
- Add a title and label the axes.

What is the range of the data on your graph?

What unit of time is being used?

Describe the change over time.

Write a question that can be answered using information from the graph.

- Copy the graph from the card on the grid.
- Add a title and label the axes.

What is the range of the data on your graph?

What unit of time is being used?

Describe the change over time.

Write a question that can be answered using information from the graph.

Figure 6.10: Sample handout for adapted lesson.

Evaluate

Table 6.7 shows the teacher's plan for the Evaluate phase of our adapted textbook lesson.

1. The teacher distributed the Performance Assessment handout to each student.

2. The teacher prompted the students to create a table of data that matches the data represented on the line graph and to explain their thinking (see fig. 6.11).

Since performance assessments allow students to respond in a variety of ways, students have both the *responsibility* and the *opportunity* to interact with the task.

HOT TIP!

If possible, enlist the support of the ESL teacher or bilingual aide for beginning and intermediate students.

Table 6.7: The Evaluate Phase of an Adapted Lesson

Content Objective	Language Objective	Study/Metacognitive Objective
Understanding	*Participating*	*Communicating*
What activity will I use to assess learning? *Daily High Temperatures performance assessment* What concept(s) will I assess? *Multiple representations of data (graph to table)* What additional skills must the students have to complete this phase successfully? *Students must be able to work backwards. That is, they must be able to transfer data from a graph to a table.* What tools and materials will students need to complete the task? *Daily High Temperatures performance assessment*	What accommodations could I include in this phase to make learning more accessible? *Students could work in pairs and then share results using chart paper.* *The activity assesses understanding of the math concepts, not reading ability; therefore, the performance assessment should be accessible to all learners.* What questions might students raise? *Do measures of time always go on the x-axis?* *Does it matter which intervals I choose?*	Student to Student *I will have students share results after everyone has completed the assessment.* Student to Teacher *Students will justify answers, either verbally or nonverbally, depending on language proficiency level.* Teacher to Student *I will ask facilitation questions as necessary.*

Use the information from the following line graph to create a table that represents the data on the graph. Explain your thinking.

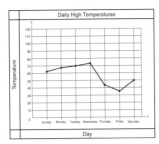

Daily High Temperatures	
Day	Temperature (in degrees Fahrenheit)
Sunday	62
Monday	67
Tuesday	70
Wednesday	73
Thursday	44
Friday	36
Saturday	50

Figure 6.11: Sample performance assessment for adapted lesson.

BIG IDEAS

- It is possible to adapt traditional lessons with just a few changes of the strategies and practices that will enhance learning.
- You don't have to do it all immediately!
- When you are comfortable, move on to another phase.

Points to Ponder

At which stage are you today in implementing the 5E model?

Considering your current stage, what could you do differently with the next lesson that would enhance student understanding, participation, and communication?

What would you like to try next?

At which stage would you like to see yourself next year?

Epilogue

Each person has an ideal, a hope, a dream which represents the soul. We must give to it the warmth of love, the light of understanding, and the essence of encouragement. **—Colby Dorr Dam**

As you will recall from the introduction, the number of English language learners in the United States and Canada is skyrocketing. Mathematics teachers have always been responsible for teaching mathematics content, including the academic language of mathematics. However, it is increasingly important that all content-area teachers provide ample opportunity for students to develop both social and academic language proficiency as they learn the course content in a positive environment that encourages student involvement. Only then will we equip our English language learners with the tools they need to reach their career and social goals.

The mathematics team at r4 Educated Solutions hopes the tools and strategies discussed in *Making Math Accessible to English Language Learners: Practical Tips and Suggestions* will help you in your efforts to make your students' hopes and dreams a reality.

BIG IDEAS

- Remind yourself of the growth you are seeing in your students.
- Remind yourself of the growth you are seeing in yourself.

Points to Ponder

What are your strengths in working with English language learners?

How can you play to your strengths?

Selected Glossary

Basic Interpersonal Communication Skills (BICS): This is the language ability required for social communication. It takes between one and three years to attain this basic level of oral proficiency.

bilingual education: Students are allowed to develop language proficiency in two languages by receiving instruction in some combination of English and the student's primary language.

cognates: These are words in English closely related to the student's primary language.

Cognitive Academic Language Proficiency (CALP): This refers to the mastery of academic language necessary for students to succeed in context-reduced and cognitively demanding content areas. It takes between five and ten years for a second-language student to perform at grade level without ELL support.

comprehensible input: This is content in which the level of language difficulty has been adapted to the student's proficiency level to enable him or her to understand.

English as a second language (ESL): This is an educational approach in which English language learners are instructed in the use of English during specific class periods of the school day. There is typically little or no use of the primary language. This phrase is sometimes used to refer to the students identified as English language learners.

English as a foreign language (EFL): This term is frequently used in Canada in addition to or interchangeably with *ESL* and refers to both learners of English and the programs that address their needs.

English language learner (ELL): This term applies to students whose first language is not English.

L1: This refers to the student's primary or native language.

L2: This refers to the student's new language—in this book, English.

limited English proficient (LEP): This term is used by the United States federal government to identify students who are not proficient enough in English to succeed in English-only classrooms.

primary language: This refers to the first language learned in the student's home.

pull-out instruction: This refers to learning when students leave the classroom for additional support to remediate, accelerate, or enhance instruction.

realia: This term describes real-life objects and artifacts used to enhance learning.

scaffolding: This is temporary support that uses questioning, manipulatives, and visuals to help the student increase his or her understanding from a basic to more complex level. The support (scaffold) is diminished little by little as the student's competency increases.

sheltered instruction: This refers to the instructional approach in which students are mainstreamed and in which the teacher uses physical activities, visual aids, and the environment to teach vocabulary for concept development in math and other subjects.

structured English immersion: This is English-only instruction in which the language is used and taught at a level appropriate to the student's ability to understand and which is supported by the use of visual aids, manipulatives, and a positive classroom environment.

English/Spanish Cognates in Math

English . . . . Spanish

English	Spanish
activity	*actividad*
acute angle	*ángulo agudo*
algebraic	*algebraico*
analyze	*analizar*
angle	*ángulo*
application	*aplicación*
apply	*aplicar*
appropriate unit	*unidad apropiada*
approximate	*aproximado*
architecture	*arquitectura*
area	*área*
art	*arte*
bar graph	*gráfica de barras*
calendar	*calendario*
capacity	*capacidad*
circle	*círculo*
circumference	*circunferencia*
common	*común*

common denominator . . . . *denominador común*

compare . . . . *comparar*

compatible . . . . *compatible*

complement (n.) . . . . *complemento*

complementary. . . . . *complementario*

composite . . . . *compuesto*

conclusion. . . . . *conclusión*

concrete . . . . *concreto*

concrete model . . . . *modelo concreto*

cone . . . . *cono*

congruent . . . . *congruente*

conjecture. . . . . *conjetura*

construct (v.). . . . . *construir*

conversion. . . . . *conversión*

convert (v.) . . . . *convertir*

coordinate. . . . . *coordenada*

cube. . . . . *cubo*

cubic unit . . . . *unidad cúbica*

cylinder. . . . . *cilindro*

data . . . . *datos*

decimal . . . . *decimal*

decision. . . . . *decisión*

demonstrate . . . . *demonstrar*

denominator . . . . *denominador*

density. . . . . *densidad*

dependent . . . . *dependiente*

describe. . . . . *describir*

diagram. . . . . *diagrama*

diameter . . . . *diámetro*

dimension . . . . *dimensión*

discipline. . . . . *disciplina*

divide (v.). . . . . *dividir*

division . . . . *división*

equal . . . . *igual*

equation . . . . *ecuación*

equivalent . . . . *equivalente*

estimate (v.) . . . . *estimar, calcular* estimation......................*estimación*

evaluate........................*evaluar*

exact...........................*exacto*

example.........................*ejemplo*

experience (n.).................*experiencia*

experimental....................*experimental*

exponent........................*exponente*

expression......................*expresión*

extend..........................*extender*

factorization...................*factorización*

factor (n.).....................*factor*

Fahrenheit......................*Fahrenheit*

figure..........................*figura*

form (n.).......................*forma*

formula.........................*fórmula*

fraction........................*fracción*

function (n.)...................*función*

generate........................*generar*

geometric.......................*geométrico*

geometric model.................*modelo geométrico*

geometry........................*geometría*

graph (n.)......................*gráfica*

graphical representation........*representación gráfica*

greatest common factor..........*máximo común factor*

hexagon.........................*hexágono*

hypotenuse......................*hipotenusa*

identify........................*identificar*

impossible......................*imposible*

incorporate.....................*incorporar*

informal........................*informal*

interpret.......................*interpretar*

intersect.......................*intersecar*

investigation...................*investigación*

iteration.......................*repetición*

language........................*lenguaje*

lateral surface area............*área lateral de la superficie*

line............................*línea*

line graph	*gráfica lineal*
logical	*lógico*
mass	*masa*
mathematics	*matemáticas*
median	*mediana*
metric	*métrico*
million	*millón*
minute	*minuto*
mode	*moda (estadísticas)*
model (n.)	*modelo*
multiple	*múltiplo*
multiplication	*multiplicación*
multiply	*multiplicar*
name	*nombre*
non-negative	*no negativos*
number pair	*par de número*
number	*número*
numerator	*numerador*
object (n.)	*objeto*
obtuse	*obtuso*
octagon	*octágono*
operation	*operación*
order (n.)	*orden*
order (v.)	*ordenar*
ordered pair	*par ordenado*
organize	*organizar*
paper (n.)	*papel*
parallel	*paralelo*
parallelogram	*paralelogramo*
pattern	*patrón*
pentagon	*pentágono*
percentage	*porcentaje*
perimeter	*perímetro*
perpendicular	*perpendicular*
physical	*físico*
pictograph	*pictografía*
picture graph	*pictografía*

plan . . . . *plan*

point (n.) . . . . *punto*

polygon . . . . *polígono*

prediction . . . . *predicción*

price . . . . *precio*

prime . . . . *primo*

prism . . . . *prisma*

probability . . . . *probabilidad*

problem . . . . *problema*

process (n.) . . . . *proceso*

product . . . . *producto*

property . . . . *propiedad*

proportion . . . . *proporcíon*

proportional . . . . *proporcional*

proportionality . . . . *proporcionalidad*

pyramid . . . . *pirámide*

Pythagorean Theorem . . . . *Teorema de Pitágoras*

quadrilateral . . . . *cuadrilátero*

quantitative . . . . *cuantitativo*

quantitative reasoning . . . . *razonamiento cuantitativo*

radius . . . . *radio*

range . . . . *rango, alcance de una función*

rational . . . . *racional*

reasonable . . . . *razonable*

reasoning . . . . *razonamiento*

rectangular prism . . . . *prisma rectangular*

reflection . . . . *reflexión*

relate (v.) . . . . *relacionar*

relation . . . . *relación*

relationship . . . . *relación*

represent . . . . *representar*

representation . . . . *representación*

result . . . . *resultado*

rhombus . . . . *rombo*

right angle . . . . *ángulo recto*

rotation . . . . *rotación*

round (v.) . . . . *redondear*

separate (adj.) . . . .*separado*

separate (v.) . . . .*separar*

sequence . . . .*secuencia*

simple event . . . .*evento simple*

situation . . . .*situación*

solution . . . .*solución*

spatial . . . .*espacial*

sphere . . . .*esfera*

statistics . . . .*estadísticas*

strategy . . . .*estrategia*

supplementary . . . .*suplementario*

symbol . . . .*símbolo*

symmetrical . . . .*simétrico*

symmetry . . . .*simetría*

systematically . . . .*sistemáticamente*

table (n.) . . . .*tabla*

technique . . . .*técnica*

technology . . . .*tecnología*

temperature . . . .*temperatura*

theoretical . . . .*teórico, hipotético*

thermometer . . . .*termómetro*

transformation . . . .*transformación*

translation . . . .*translación*

transversal . . . .*transversal*

trapezoid . . . .*trapecio*

triangle . . . .*triángulo*

triangular . . . .*triangular*

triangular prism . . . .*prísma triangular*

triangular pyramid . . . .*pirámide triangular*

unit . . . .*unidad*

validate . . . .*validar*

validity . . . .*validez*

variable . . . .*variable*

vertex . . . .*vértice*

vocabulary . . . .*vocabulario*

volume . . . .*volumen*

Sample Responses to Tasks and Reflections

Reflection 1.1

Some students transition to English very quickly because they are eager to learn, have supportive families, and are encouraged by teachers who care and provide appropriate instruction and a welcoming environment.

Task: Identifying Language Proficiency Levels

Case Study: Anh

Early intermediate

Possible indicators:

- Attempts to speak English but relies heavily on gestures and facial expressions
- Becomes frustrated when solving word problems
- Some understanding of the lesson vocabulary and concepts

Case Study: Luca

Proficient

Possible indicators:

- Understands and uses academic language
- Demonstrates understanding of abstract mathematical concepts

- Functions on grade level
- Uses advanced sentence structure, including academic language, in justifying answers

Case Study: Pakiza

Beginning

Possible indicators:

- Relies on pictures, gestures, and translations
- Does not demonstrate that she understands the problem

Case Study: Camilo

Advanced

Possible indicators:

- Can read unmodified texts, although he may occasionally need assistance
- Performs well enough to pass reading and math assessments (writing usually more difficult than reading)
- Communicates understanding of mathematical concepts on grade level

Case Study: Lin

Intermediate

Possible indicators:

- Relies on modified texts
- Receives family support, which contributes to accelerated language and content acquisition
- Asks for assistance (beginning students rarely ask for assistance)

Reflection 1.2

Beginning student:

- Challenge for student—Staying focused, having any idea about what is going on
- Challenge for teacher—How can I help him or her understand the math when he or she doesn't understand anything I am saying?

Early intermediate student:

- Challenge for student—Understanding only a few words and misapplying, which results in misconceptions
- Challenge for teacher—Because the student thinks he or she understands but may not, the teacher incorrectly thinks the student "got it."

Intermediate student:

- Challenge for student—Deciding what is important information in word problems
- Challenge for teacher—Helping student develop math vocabulary

Advanced student:

- Challenge for student—Understanding the dense, complex structure of word problems
- Challenge for teacher—The student can solve problems with straightforward text, but how do I help him or her decode more complex problems?

Proficient student:

- Challenge for student—Understanding the idioms and subtleties of the English language
- Challenge for teacher—Helping the student "fine tune" English and demonstrate mathematical proficiency at a high level of cognitive rigor

Reflection 2.1

- Being greeted by my friendly teacher at the door
- Being included in classroom activities
- The teacher and/or students saying something in my first language

Reflection 2.2

- I face the class when speaking, create an attractive classroom, and am patient, kind, and understanding.
- I make a conscious effort to repeat important information and to pronounce students' names correctly.
- I will start labeling objects and provide more wait time.

Task: Choosing Appropriate Affective Practices

Anh:

- Smile.
- Speak slowly and distinctly using simplified language.
- Allow audio recording of lessons.
- Use flexible grouping. (Because she is shy, she would probably participate more in a small group than with the whole class.)

Luca:

- Avoid slang and explain idioms. (For example, *to get out on the wrong side of the bed* is to be in a bad mood.)
- Use flexible grouping. (He could be a good group leader.)
- Have groups present work on chart paper. (Encourage expression of ideas using descriptive language and multiple representations of math concepts.)

Pakiza:

- Label objects, speak slowly and distinctly, allow audio recordings, and ask for thumbs up/thumbs down responses to ease her transition to English.
- Find opportunities to bring the student's culture and language into class. (Because she has a strong tie to family and friends, providing connections to her community may increase her interest in class.)
- Use flexible grouping. (Because she is very social, working with others and developing classroom friends may appeal to her.)

Camilo:

- Use frequent, genuine praise. (This praise will help build his confidence to enhance communication skills.)
- Create word walls. (Include academic vocabulary to build mathematics language skills in addition to his social language skills.)
- Have students present work on chart paper. (This provides opportunities for both collaboration and feedback to increase communication of math concepts.)

Lin:

- Allow audio recording so he can replay what he has heard. Since he has strong family support, they may be able to use the recordings to support his learning at home.
- Provide word banks and sentence stems to encourage him to speak and write.
- Encourage him to make and add to a personal dictionary of new terms.

Reflection 2.3

I would be motivated to learn the language as quickly as possible. I also have a well-developed primary language as well as the cognitive ability to learn a new language relatively easily. I would also have access to the language and the means to take advantage of the available resources.

Task: Aligning Affective Practices to Second Language Acquisition Factors

Practice	Motivation	Age	Access to the Language	Personality	First Language Development	Cognitive Ability	Effective Instruction
Smile.	X						X
Pronounce the student's name correctly.	X						X
Be sure the student knows your name.	X						X
Establish routines so students know what to expect.	X		X				X
Face the class when speaking.			X				X
Speak slowly and distinctly.			X				X
Avoid slang and explain idioms.			X				X
Write legibly.			X				X
Repeat important information.			X				X
Allow students to audio record lessons.			X				X
Label objects in the classroom, such as *trash* and *overhead projector*.			X				X
Create attractive, content-related bulletin boards.			X				X
Provide plenty of wait time.	X		X				X
Be patient, kind, understanding, and friendly.	X						X
Teach to appeal to all five senses.			X				X
Create a positive, nonthreatening classroom environment.	X		X				X
Create a nurturing environment.	X		X				X
Find opportunities to bring the student's culture and language into class.	X		X				X
Give frequent, genuine praise.	X		X				X
Post procedures and schedules.	X		X				X
Use flexible grouping.	X		X				X
Assign bilingual students as peer partners.	X		X				X
Have groups present work using chart paper and markers.	X		X				X
Highlight contributions of mathematicians from other cultures.	X		X				X
Create word walls.			X				X
Use personal response boards, which can be easily cut from bathroom tileboard.	X		X				X
Ask for thumbs up/thumbs down or other physical responses.	X		X				X

Reflection 2.4

Teachers have no influence over the student's age, first language development, or cognitive ability. To some extent, the teacher can influence student motivation with kindness, understanding, a nurturing classroom environment, and, perhaps to a more limited extent, even personality. The teacher has greater influence over access to English while the student is in the classroom, but the factor over which teachers have the greatest influence is effectiveness of instruction.

Task: Determining Linguistic Obstacles

Beginning:

- The problem seems to be incomprehensible, with the exception of numerals and very common words.

Early intermediate:

- The student seems to understand only very basic general vocabulary.
- The student may understand *skirt* and *sweater* only because of the graphics.
- The student does not understand pronouns, prepositions, and verb tenses.

Intermediate:

- The student still has a limited vocabulary.
- Pronouns, prepositions, and verb tenses still present a challenge.

Advanced:

- Prepositions may still confuse students at this proficiency level.
- The student is still acquiring some grade-appropriate vocabulary.
- *All different combinations* may still be unfamiliar to advanced students.
- It is not important that she is purchasing an outfit for her piano recital, but students may not be able to filter out unnecessary information.

Proficient:

- There are few, varying by student.

Reflection 3.1

Responses will vary.

Task: Creating a Vocabulary Organizer

Responses will vary.

Task: Choosing Appropriate Linguistic Strategies

Anh:

- Vocabulary organizers
- Word sorts
- Find Someone Who

Luca:

- Vocabulary organizers
- Concept definition maps
- Word sorts
- Think-alouds
- Find Someone Who

Pakiza:

- Vocabulary organizer (with group or partner)
- Word sorts (with group or partner)
- Find Someone Who (with group or partner)

Camilo:

- Vocabulary organizers
- Concept definition maps
- Cognates
- Word sorts
- Think-alouds
- Find Someone Who

Lin:

- Vocabulary organizers
- Concept definition maps
- Word sorts
- Think-alouds
- Find Someone Who

Reflection 3.2

I will use the vocabulary organizer continually to create an expanding word wall. I also have several beginning Spanish-speaking students. I will use the cognates with them.

Task: Determining Mathematical Obstacles

Beginning: No. He or she cannot understand the mathematical concepts needed to solve the problem.

Early intermediate: Probably not. He or should would likely perform a random arithmetic operation using numbers from the problem.

Intermediate: Possibly, especially if general vocabulary has been pretaught.

Advanced: Probably, especially since there is a graphic.

Proficient: Yes. There is enough information to expect the student to solve the problem.

Reflection 4.1

Sometimes students "zone out." Some students avoid the situation by not coming to school or finding reasons to leave class. Others talk to their friends that speak the same language. Some students get answers from other students, while others just don't do the work.

Task: Choosing Appropriate Tools and Activities

Student Name	Activity	Manipulatives	Example/ Nonexample	Who Am I?	Window Panes	Four-Quadrant Problem Solver	See-Plan-Do-Reflect	Bonded Brains
Anh	Understanding	Color tiles	✓	✓	✓			
	Participating		✓	✓	✓			✓
	Communicating				✓	✓	✓	✓
Luca	Understanding	Color tiles	✓	✓	✓			
	Participating		✓	✓	✓			✓
	Communicating				✓	✓	✓	✓
Pakiza	Understanding	Color tiles	✓	✓	✓			
	Participating		✓	✓	✓			✓
	Communicating				✓	✓	✓	✓
Camilo	Understanding	Color tiles	✓	✓	✓			
	Participating		✓	✓	✓			✓
	Communicating				✓	✓	✓	✓
Lin	Understanding	Color tiles	✓	✓	✓			
	Participating		✓	✓	✓			✓
	Communicating				✓	✓	✓	✓

Reflection 4.2

The unit appears to involve perimeter and area. If I had all five students in the same class, I would have students use manipulatives, especially the color tiles, while they worked in groups to understand the difference between perimeter and area. As they arrange the tiles in different ways, they can discover that they can make different rectangles. I would use example/nonexamples with them afterwards to reinforce the concept and be sure they understood the difference. They could use the window-pane activity as another way to communicate since they can draw pictures. Then they could use Bonded Brains to share their findings. For the performance assessment, I would encourage them to use either the four-quadrant problem solver or See-Plan-Do-Reflect to help them organize their work. These strategies would probably help all of my students, including those with special needs.

Task: Using Rubrics for Evaluation

Note that even though students may not solve the problem correctly, conceptual and procedural knowledge and communication improve as the student's language proficiency increases.

Anh

Student arrived at a correct solution:	Yes	(No)		
	4	3	2	1
Conceptual knowledge			✓	
Procedural knowledge			✓	
Communication skills			✓	

Luca

Student arrived at a correct solution:	(Yes)	No		
	4	3	2	1
Conceptual knowledge	✓			
Procedural knowledge	✓			
Communication skills	✓			

Pakiza

Student arrived at a correct solution:	Yes	(No)		
	4	3	2	1
Conceptual knowledge				✓
Procedural knowledge				✓
Communication skills				✓

Camilo

Student arrived at a correct solution: Yes No				
	4	3	2	1
Conceptual knowledge	✓			
Procedural knowledge	✓			
Communication skills		✓		

Lin

Student arrived at a correct solution: Yes No				
	4	3	2	1
Conceptual knowledge	✓			
Procedural knowledge	✓			
Communication skills			✓	

D

Reproducibles
for Lesson on Investigating
Transformations

Tangram Masters (2 Sets)

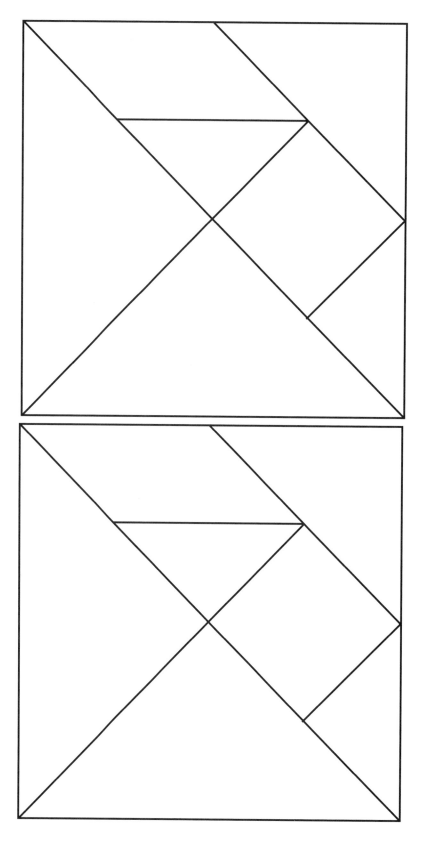

Reflection Path Activity Card

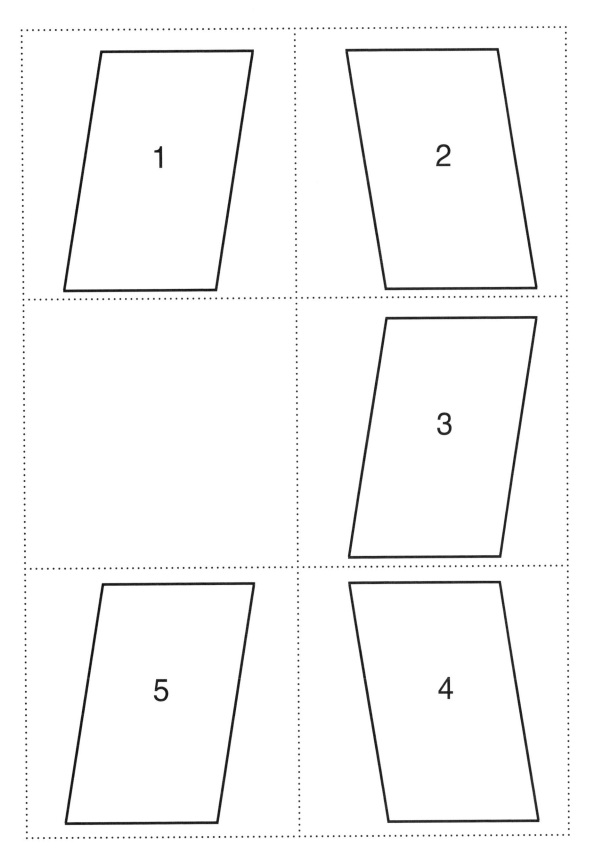

Rotation Path Activity Card

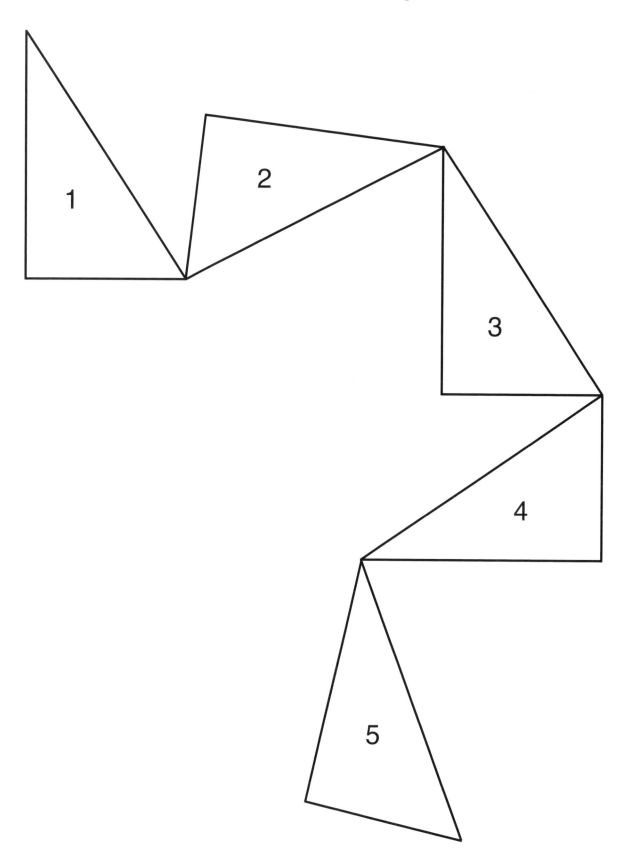

Translation Path Activity Card

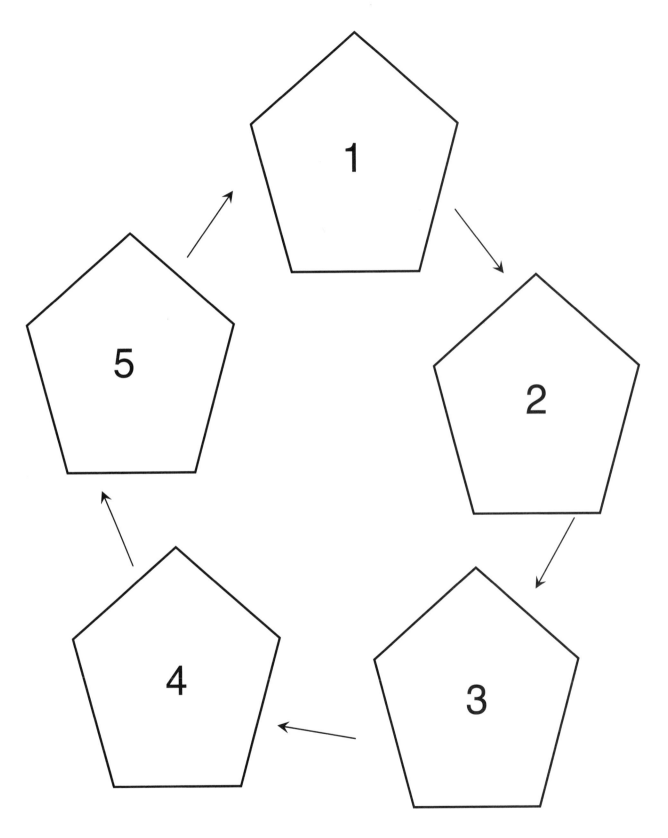

Transformation Paths Shapes (2 Sets)

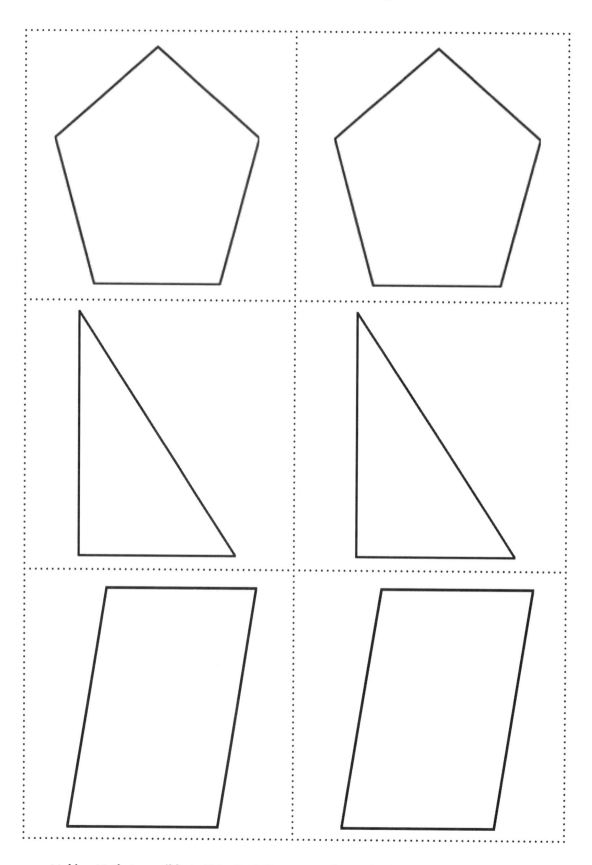

Transformation Path Activity Card

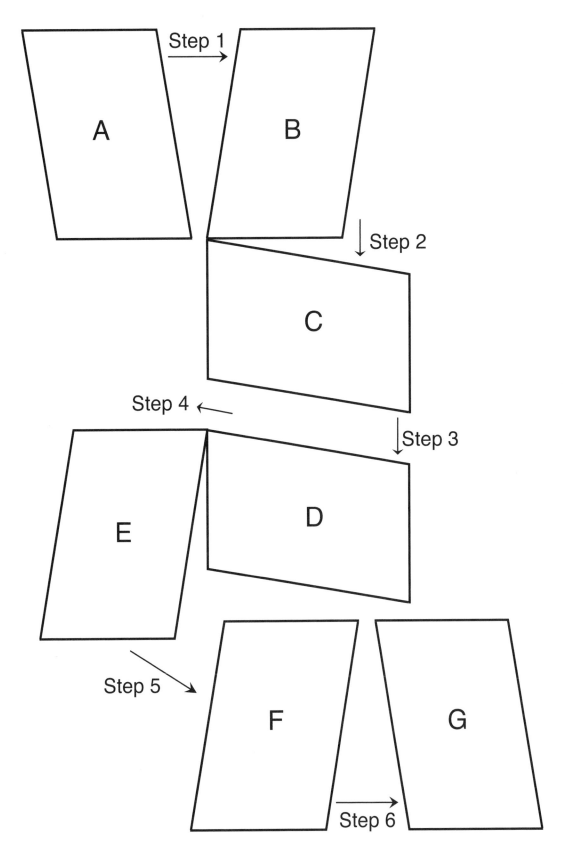

Transformation Path Directions

Step 1 Describe how you moved the shape. Name the transformation. Explain your thinking.	**Step 4** Describe how you moved the shape. Name the transformation. Explain your thinking.
Step 2 Describe how you moved the shape. Name the transformation. Explain your thinking.	**Step 5** Describe how you moved the shape. Name the transformation. Explain your thinking.
Step 3 Describe how you moved the shape. Name the transformation. Explain your thinking.	**Step 6** Describe how you moved the shape. Name the transformation. Explain your thinking.

Transformation Match-Up Cards

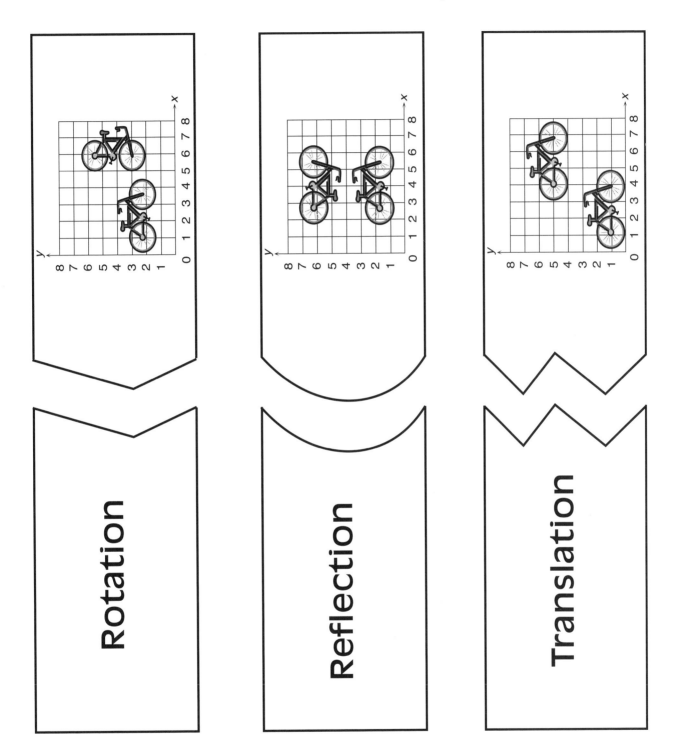

Rotation

Reflection

Translation

Symmetrical Transformations Page 1

1. Complete. Trace. Represent a rotation.

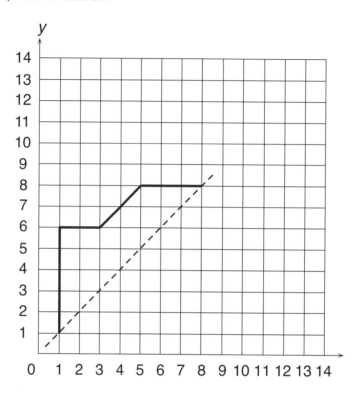

2. Complete. Trace. Represent a reflection.

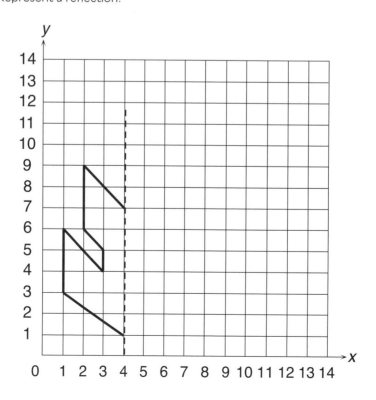

Symmetrical Transformations Page 2

1. Complete. Trace. Represent a translation.

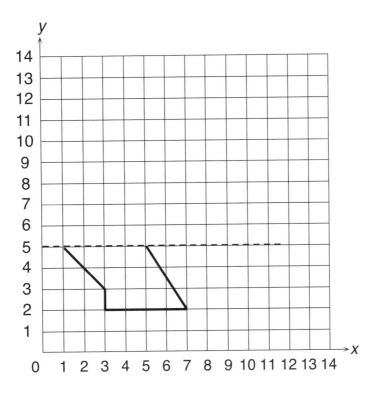

2. Complete. Trace. Represent a _____. (your choice)

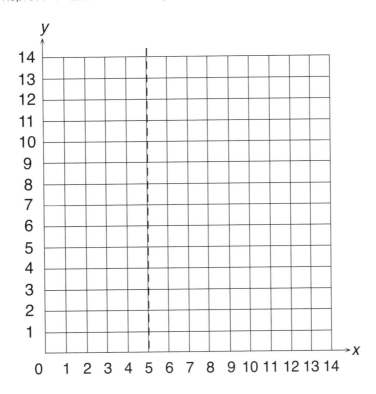

Symmetry Sort Cards

Symmetry Sort Mat

One Line of Symmetry	More Than One Line of Symmetry	No Line of Symmetry

Vocabulary Organizer

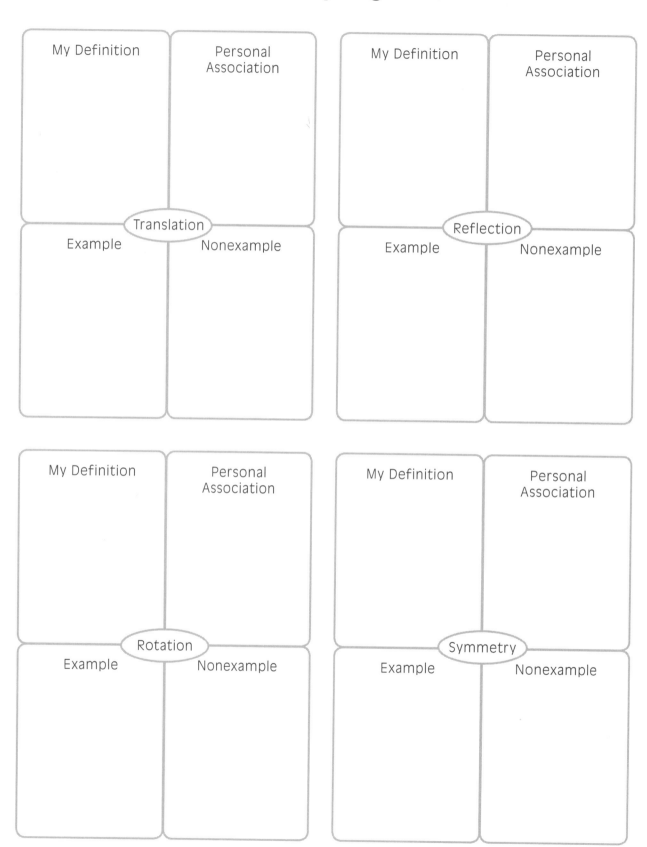

My Definition	Personal Association
Example	Nonexample

Translation

My Definition	Personal Association
Example	Nonexample

Reflection

My Definition	Personal Association
Example	Nonexample

Rotation

My Definition	Personal Association
Example	Nonexample

Symmetry

Performance Assessment

Create a design using the pattern blocks shown below, and record it on the grid. Show a translation of your design. Record the translation of your design on the grid, and shade the translated design. Explain your thinking.

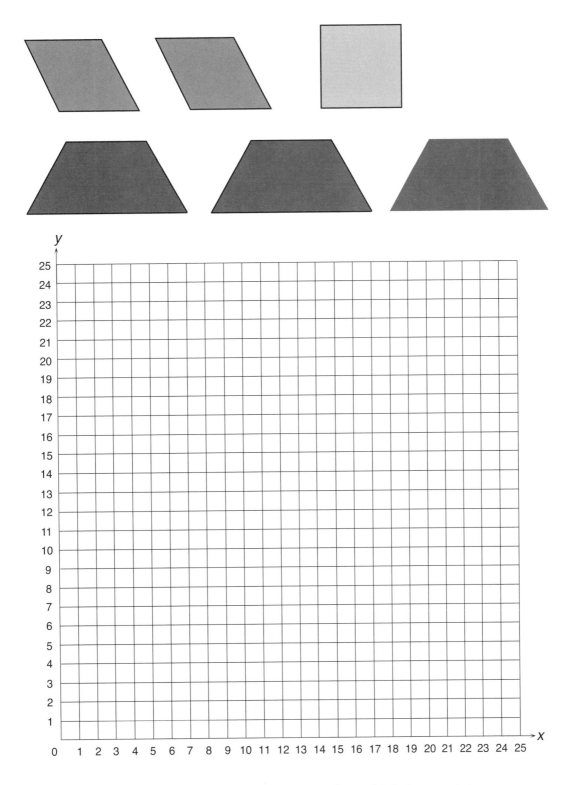

Cooperative Grouping for the ELL Classroom

Advanced Preparation

- Copy, cut, and glue the grouping shapes on page 171 to index cards.
- Cut teacher cue cards (page 172).
- Laminate index cards and teacher cue cards to make them last longer.

How to Use

Assign Cooperative Grouping Cards based on the student's ability level, using the following guide, for example:

- Beginning and early intermediate English language learners—bear
- Intermediate English language learners—zebra
- Advanced English language learners—lion
- Proficient English language learners—giraffe

Cards will need to be reassigned every two to three weeks based on the amount of cooperative grouping used during the time frame and the changing dynamics of the classroom. For example, the beginning English language learners could be changed to the zebra.

Teacher cue cards will help facilitate smooth group transitions and aid the beginning learners in the classroom.

HOT TIP!

1. Using your seating chart and a second set of grouping shapes, put tape on the back of the symbols, and attach them to students' assigned seat positions.

2. Attach the grouping shape to the student's desk or seat position during the duration of the two- to three-week period.

Possible Groupings by ELL Classification

Ability groups: Group by animal (groups of two, three, and four can be used).

Semirandom groups:

- Pairs—Group by number. Create pairs between students who are two levels apart. For example, pair a beginning/early intermediate student with an advanced student.

- Trios—Group by letter. Each group should contain three different ability levels.

- Groups of four—Group by animal. The groups will contain one student at each ability level.

Mixed groups: Distribute the set of grouping shapes randomly, and group as follows.

- Groups of two—Group by number.

- Groups of three—Group by letter.

- Groups of four—Group by animal.

Cooperative Grouping Guide Cards

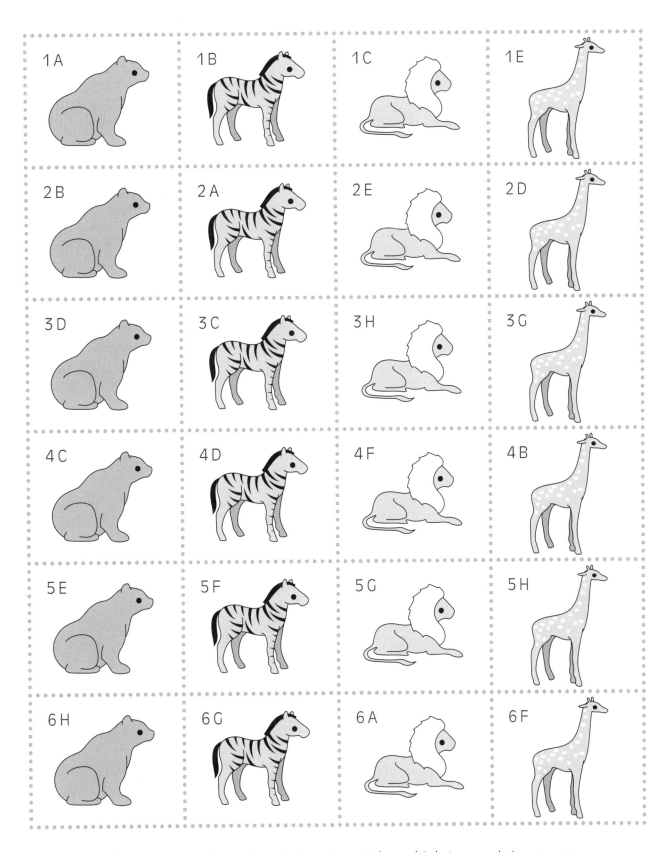

Teacher Cue Cards

Animals

Use for groups of four. Assign one animal to each level.

- Beginning and early intermediate English language learners
- Intermediate English language learners
- Advanced English language learners
- Proficient English language learners

Letters

Use for groups of three. Assign a letter for each of four ability levels.

Numbers

Use for pairs. Create pairs between students who are two levels apart.

- Beginning and early intermediate with advanced
- Intermediate with proficient

A 5E Lesson Plan Template

A 5E Lesson Plan Template

Learning Phase	Content Objective *Understanding*	Language Objective *Participating*	Study/Metacognitive Objective *Communicating*
Engage	• What activity will I use to stimulate curiosity and activate prior knowledge? • What tools and materials are needed for this activity? • What prior knowledge do I want to activate? • What nonconceptual vocabulary do I need to preteach?	• What accommodations could I include in this phase to make learning more accessible? • What questions might students raise?	• Student to Student • Student to Teacher • Teacher to Student • Facilitation Questions
Explore	• What concept(s) will students explore? • What activity will I use to encourage students to explore the concept(s)? • What tools or materials will allow students to become directly involved in exploring the concept(s)? • What vocabulary and symbols do students need to understand for this phase?	• What accommodations could I include in this phase to make learning more accessible? • What questions might students raise?	• Student to Student • Student to Teacher • Teacher to Student • Facilitation Questions
Explain	• What misconceptions do I anticipate that may need to be corrected? • How will I develop conceptual vocabulary? • What connections are essential for the student to understand? • What algorithms (computational procedures) are connected to the concept? • What new vocabulary is introduced?	• What accommodations could I include in this phase to make learning more accessible? • What questions might students raise?	• Student to Student • Student to Teacher • Teacher to Student • Facilitation Questions
Elaborate	• What activity will I use to expand or elaborate on the concept(s)? • What tools or materials are needed for this activity? • What new vocabulary will students need for this phase of the lesson? • How will I encourage the use of vocabulary? • What concepts and processes must students understand to be successful with this phase of the lesson? • How (if at all) must the algorithms (computational procedures) be applied?	• What accommodations could I include in this phase to make learning more accessible? • What questions might students raise?	• Student to Student • Student to Teacher • Teacher to Student • Facilitation Questions
Evaluate	• What activity will I use to assess learning? • What concept(s) will I assess? • What additional skills must the students have to complete this phase successfully? • What tools and materials will students need to complete the task?	• What accommodations could I include in this phase to make learning more accessible? • What questions might students raise?	• Student to Student • Student to Teacher • Teacher to Student

References and Resources

Abedi, J. (2004). The No Child Left Behind Act and English language learners: Assessment and accountability issues. *Educational Researcher, 33*(1), 4–14.

Barton, M., & Heidema, C. (2002). *Teaching reading in mathematics* (2nd ed.). Aurora, CO: Mid-continent Research for Education and Learning.

Batt, L., Kim, J., & Sunderman, G. (2005). *Limited English proficient students: Increased accountability under NCLB—A policy brief.* Cambridge, MA: Harvard University.

Bye, M. P. (1975). *Reading in mathematics and cognitive development.* Unpublished manuscript. (ERIC Document Reproduction Service No. ED124926)

Camarota, S. A. (2007). *Immigrants in the United States, 2007.* Center for Immigration Studies. Accessed at www.cis.org/articles/2007/back1007.html on February 14, 2009.

Canada Department of Justice. (1988). *Canadian Multiculturalism Act.* Accessed at http://laws.justice.gc.ca/en/ShowFullDoc/cs/c-18.7 on February 16, 2009.

Capps, R., Fix, M. E., & Murray, J. (2005). *The new demography of America's schools: Immigration and the No Child Left Behind Act.* Washington, DC: Urban Institute. Accessed at www.urban.org on January 20, 2009.

Centre for Canadian Language Benchmarks. (n.d.). *Frequently asked questions (FAQ).* Accessed at www.language.ca/display_page.asp?page_id=253 on February 15, 2009.

Child Trends Data Bank. (n.d.). *Dropout rates.* Accessed at www.childtrendsdatabank. org/indicators/1HighSchoolDropout.cfm on February 15, 2009.

Coalition for Equal Access to Education. (2009). *Roles of stakeholders.* Accessed at www.eslaction.com/index.php?page=stakeholders on February 16, 2009.

Council of Ministers of Education, Canada. (2007). *Pan-Canadian Assessment Program, 2007: Reading, mathematics, and science highlights.* Accessed at www.cmec.ca/pcap/2007/PCAP2007-highlights.en.pdf on February 16, 2009.

Council of Ministers of Education, Canada. (2008). *Education in Canada.* Accessed at www.cmec.ca/international/educationcanada.en.pdf on February 16, 2009.

Crandall, J., Dale, T. C., Rhodes, N. C., & Spanos, G. A. (1985, October). *The language of mathematics: The English barrier.* Paper presented at the Seventh Delaware Symposium on Language Studies, Newark, DE.

Cummins, J. (1981). The role of primary language development in promoting educational success for language minority students. In Office of Bilingual Bicultural Education, California State Department of Education, *Schooling and language minority students: A theoretical framework* (pp. 3–49). Los Angeles: California State University.

Dale, T. C., & Cuevas, G. J. (1992). Integrating mathematics and language learning. In P. A. Richard-Amato & M. A. Snow (Eds.), *The multicultural classroom: Readings for content-area teachers* (pp. 58–70). White Plains, NY: Longman.

Davey, B. (1983). Think aloud: Modeling the cognitive processes of reading comprehension. *Journal of Reading, 27*(1), 44–47.

Echevarria, J., & Graves, A. (1998). *Sheltered content instruction.* Boston: Allyn & Bacon.

Echevarria, J., Vogt, J., & Short, D. (2004). *Making content comprehensible for English learners.* Boston: Pearson Education.

Genesee, F., & Gándara, P. (1999). Bilingual education programs: A cross-national perspective. *Journal of Social Issues, 55*(4), 665–685.

Gunderson, L. (2008). Commentary: The state of the art of secondary ESL teaching and learning. *Journal of Adolescent & Adult Literacy, 52*(3), 184–188. Accessed at www.reading.org/Library/OldRetrieve.cfm?jaal-52-3-gunderson.pdf&D=10.1598/JAAL.52.3.1&F=JAAL-52-3-Gunderson.pdf on February 15, 2009.

Halliday, M. (1978). *Language as social semiotic: The social interpretation of language and meaning.* Baltimore, MD: University Park Press.

Haynes, J. (2003). *Challenges for ELLs in content area learning.* Accessed at www.everythingesl.net on January 20, 2009.

He, C. (2008). *What is ESL?* Accessed at www.youthcanada.ca/article/what-esl on February 11, 2009.

Jarrett, D. (1999). *The inclusive classroom: Teaching mathematics and science to English language learners—It's just good teaching.* Portland, OR: Northwest Regional Educational Laboratory.

Kessler, C. (1985, October). *Processing mathematics in a second language: Problems for LEP children.* Paper presented at the Seventh Delaware Symposium on Language Studies, Newark, DE.

Krashen, S. D. (1982). *Principles and practice in second language acquisition.* New York: Prentice Hall.

Krashen, S. D. (1985). *Insights and inquiries: Second language teaching immersion and bilingual education literacy.* Hayward, CA: Alemany.

Marzano, R. (2001). *Classroom instruction that works.* Alexandria, VA: Association for Supervision and Curriculum Development.

McLaughlin, M. (1993). *A classroom guide to performance-based assessment.* Princeton, NJ: Houghton-Mifflin.

McLaughlin, M., & Vogt, M. (1996). *Portfolios in teacher education.* Newark, DE: International Reading Association.

National Association for Bilingual Education. (2006, July). *What is bilingual education?* Accessed at www.nabe.org/education/index.html on January 20, 2009.

National Center for Education Statistics. (n.d.). *Characteristics of the 100 largest public elementary and secondary school districts in the United States: 2003–04.* Accessed at http://nces.ed.gov/pubs2006/100_largest/tables/table_a12.asp on June 18, 2009.

National Clearinghouse for English Language Acquisition and Language Instruction Educational Programs. (n.d.). *English language proficiency assessment(s) used by each state in 2005–06, with contact information.* Accessed at www.ncela.gwu.edu/expert/faq/25tests.htm on February 25, 2009.

National Council of Teachers of Mathematics. (2000). *Principles and standards for school mathematics.* Reston, VA: Author.

National Council of Teachers of Mathematics. (2005). *A position paper: Closing the achievement gap.* Reston, VA: Author.

National Research Council. (2001). The strands of mathematical proficiency. In National Research Council (Ed.), *Adding it up: Helping children learn mathematics* (pp. 115–156). Washington, DC: National Academy Press.

National Research Council. (2002). *Helping children learn mathematics.* Washington, DC: National Academies Press.

National Symposium on Learning Disabilities in English Language Learners. (2003, October). *Symposium summary.* Accessed at http://ed.gov/about/offices/list/osers/products/ld-ell/index.html on January 20, 2009.

Polya, G. (1957). *How to solve it.* Princeton, NJ: Princeton University Press.

r4 Educated Solutions. (2004a). *TAKS mathematics preparation: Grade 1.* Houston, TX: Author.

r4 Educated Solutions. (2004b). *TAKS mathematics preparation: Grade 11 exit.* Houston, TX: Author.

r4 Educated Solutions. (2005). *Accelerated curriculum: Grade 11 exit.* Houston, TX: Author.

Reehm, S. P., & Long, S. A. (1996). Reading in the mathematics classroom. *Middle School Journal, 27*(5), 35–41.

Romo, H. (1993). *Mexican immigrants in high schools: Meeting their needs.* Charleston, WV: ERIC Clearinghouse on Rural Education and Small Schools. (ERIC Document Reproduction Service No. ED357905)

Ruiz-de-Velasco, J., & Fix, M. (2000). *Overlooked and underserved: Immigrant students in U.S. secondary schools.* Washington, DC: Urban Institute. Accessed at www.urban.org on January 20, 2009.

Secada, W. G., & de la Cruz, Y. (1996). *Teaching mathematics for understanding to bilingual students.* Charleston, WV: ERIC Clearinghouse on Rural Education and Small Schools. (ERIC Document Reproduction Service No. ED393646)

Schumann, J. H. (1978). *The pidginization process: A model for second language acquisition.* Rowley, MA: Newbury House.

Statistics Canada. (1994). *Report on the demographic situation in Canada.* Accessed at www.statcan.gc.ca/pub/91-209-x/91-209-x1994000-eng.pdf on February 14, 2009.

Statistics Canada. (2001). *Population and dwelling counts, for Canada, provinces and territories, 1991 and 1996 censuses.* Accessed at www.statcan.gc.ca/c1996-r1996/4129974-eng.htm on February 10, 2009.

Statistics Canada. (2006). *Population by language spoken most often at home and age group.* Accessed at www12.statcan.ca/english/census06/data/highlights/language/Table402.cfm on February 10, 2009.

Stiggins, R. (1970). *Student-centered classroom assessment.* Upper Saddle River, NJ: Prentice Hall.

Trowbridge, L., & Bybee, R. (1996). *Teaching secondary school science: Strategies for developing literacy.* Englewood, Cliffs, NJ: Merrill.

U.S. Census Bureau. (2003). *Language use and English-speaking ability: 2000—Census 2000 brief.* Washington, DC: Author.

U.S. Department of Education. (2001). *Public law print of PL 107-110, the No Child Left Behind Act of 2001.* Accessed at www.ed.gov/policy/elsec/leg/esea02/107-110.pdf on January 20, 2009.

U.S. Department of Education. (2003). *Title I—Improving the academic achievement of the disadvantaged; final rule.* Accessed at www.ed.gov/legislation/FedRegister/finrule/2003-4/120903a.pdf on January 20, 2009.

Vygotsky, L. (1978). *Mind in society: The development of higher psychological processes.* Cambridge, MA: Harvard University.

Watt, D., & Roessingh, H. (2001). The dynamics of ESL dropout: *Plus ça change . . . Canadian Modern Language Review, 58*(2), 203–222.

Wiggins, G. (1998). *Educative assessments: Designing assessments to inform and improve student performance.* San Francisco: Jossey-Bass.

Index

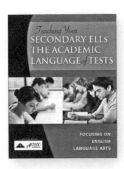

Teaching Your Secondary English Language Learners the Academic Language of Tests: Focusing on English Language Arts
By r4 Educated Solutions

Teach your English language learners unfamiliar language features before they are encountered in core content areas and standardized test questions. Evidence-based, teacher-friendly lesson plans also support content-area teachers in providing instruction for content-specific language skills. **BKF292**

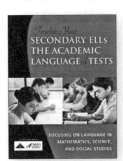

Teaching Your Secondary English Language Learners the Academic Language of Tests: Focusing on Language in Mathematics, Science, and Social Studies
By r4 Educated Solutions

Teach your English language learners unfamiliar language features before they are encountered in core content areas and standardized test questions. Evidence-based, teacher-friendly lesson plans also support content-area teachers in providing instruction for content-specific language skills. **BKF293**

Making Math Accessible to Students With Special Needs: Practical Tips and Suggestions
By r4 Educated Solutions

These manuals offer grade-appropriate research-based strategies for increasing confidence and capability among students with special needs. Reflective questions and tasks make this a perfect book for self-guided or group study. Appendices offer sample answers and additional supports.
Grades K–2: **BKF288** Grades 3–5: **BKF289** Grades 6–8: **BKF290** Grades 9–12: **BKF291**

Pyramid Response to Intervention: RTI, Professional Learning Communities, and How to Respond When Kids Don't Learn
Austin Buffum, Mike Mattos, and Chris Weber
Foreword by Richard DuFour

Accessible language and compelling stories illustrate how RTI is most effective when built on the Professional Learning Communities at Work™ model. Written by award-winning educators, this book details three tiers of interventions—from basic to intensive—and includes implementation ideas. **BKF251**

Understanding Response to Intervention: A Practical Guide to Systemic Implementation
Robert Howell, Sandra Patton, and Margaret Deiotte

Whether you want a basic understanding of RTI or desire thorough knowledge for district-level implementation, you need this book. Understand the nuts and bolts of RTI. Follow clear examples of effective practices that include systems and checklists to assess your RTI progress. **BKF253**

Solution Tree | Press   a division of Solution Tree   Visit solution-tree.com or call 800.733.6786 to order.

Solution Tree | Press

a division of

Solution Tree

Solution Tree's mission is to advance the work of our authors. By working with the best researchers and educators worldwide, we strive to be the premier provider of innovative publishing, in-demand events, and inspired professional development designed to transform education to ensure that all students learn.

The core purpose of Region 4 is revolutionizing education to inspire and advance future generations.™ Instructional materials such as this publication are written and reviewed by content-area specialists who have an array of experience in providing quality, effective classroom instruction that provides the most impact on student achievement.